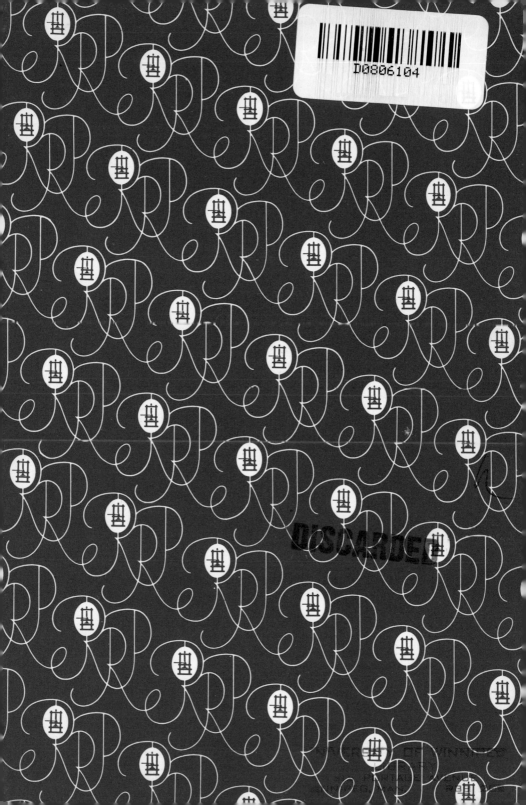

BROWNING'S DUKE

Robert Browning in 1845 (Drawing by E. Heber Thompson).

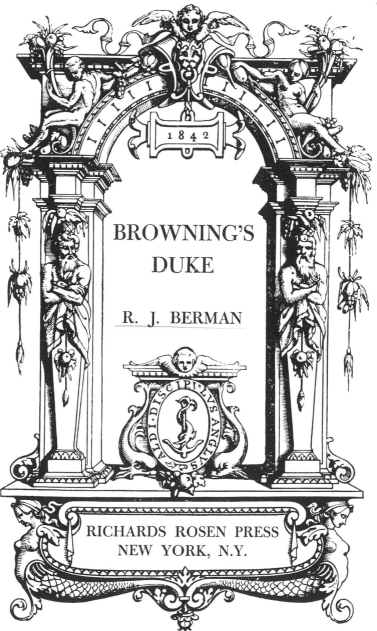

1842

BROWNING'S DUKE

R. J. BERMAN

ALDI·DISCIPLVS·ANGLVS

RICHARDS ROSEN PRESS
NEW YORK, N.Y.

Standard Book Number: 8239–0247–1
Library of Congress Catalog Card Number: 72–167641

Published in 1972 by Richards Rosen Press, Inc.
29 East 21st Street, New York City, N.Y. 10010

First Edition
Manufactured in the United States of America

Dedication

To my Mother and Father

Acknowledgments

The author wishes to thank the Academic Committee at the Horace Mann School, and especially Dr. Harry H. Williams and Philip D. Lewerth, for a generous grant that enabled him to complete this study. He is also grateful to Dr. Sallie Jo Strouss of Horace Mann and Lt. Stephen D. Barney of Rome for their help in securing data relevant to the paintings of Alfonso II d'Este and Lucrezia de' Medici d'Este. Special thanks should go to Robert Cullen of Horace Mann for his valuable suggestions during the writing of the present study.

For permission to quote from certain sources, acknowledgments are due to dall'Oglio Editore, Milano, for Chiappini's *Gli Estensi*; Octagon Books, New York, for Smith's *Browning's Star-Imagery*; The University of Kentucky Press, for Fairchild's "Browning the Simple-Hearted Casuist" and Perrine's "Browning's Shrewd Duke"; Appleton-Century-Crofts, New York, for Brooks, Purser, and Warren's *An Approach to Literature*; The University of New Mexico Press, for Crowell's *The Triple Soul: Browning's Theory of Knowledge*; The University of Western Australia Press, for Burrows' *Browning the Poet: An Introductory Study*; Bobbs-Merrill and Archon Books, New York, for Phelps's *Robert Browning*; Eyre and Spottiswoode, London, for

Blackburn's *Robert Browning: A Study of His Poetry*; Oliver &
Boyd, Edinburgh and London, for Cadbury's "Lyric and Anti-
Lyric Forms: A Method for Judging Browning"; *Victorian
Newsletter,* for Stevens' "My Last Duchess': A Possible Source"
and Millets' "Art and Reality in 'My Last Duchess'"; *The Ex-
plicator* for Kilburns' "Browning's *My Last Duchess*"; *Victorian
Poetry,* for Fleissner's "Browning's Last Lost Duchess: A Pur-
view," and Monteiro's "Browning's 'My Last Duchess'"; and to
The College Language Association Journal, for Cox's "The 'Spot
of Joy' in 'My Last Duchess.'"

About the Author

R. J. BERMAN is a graduate of the University of Michigan and holds an M.A. from Columbia University. He has studied also at Oxford and the University of Florence. Since 1960 Mr. Berman has been at the Horace Mann School in New York City, where he teaches courses in Victorian Literature, Russian Literature, Milton, and Melville.

Contents

MY LAST DUCHESS

FERRARA

1	That's my last Duchess painted on the wall,
2	Looking as if she were alive. I call
3	That piece a wonder, now: Frà Pandolf's hands
4	Worked busily a day, and there she stands.
5	Will't please you sit and look at her? I said
6	"Frà Pandolf" by design, for never read
7	Strangers like you that pictured countenance,
8	The depth and passion of its earnest glance,
9	But to myself they turned (since none puts by
10	The curtain I have drawn for you, but I)
11	And seemed as they would ask me, if they durst,
12	How such a glance came there; so, not the first
13	Are you to turn and ask thus. Sir, 'twas not
14	Her husband's presence only, called that spot
15	Of joy into the Duchess' cheek: perhaps
16	Frà Pandolf chanced to say "Her mantle laps
17	Over my lady's wrist too much," or "Paint
18	Must never hope to reproduce the faint
19	Half-flush that dies along her throat:" such stuff
20	Was courtesy, she thought, and cause enough
21	For calling up that spot of joy. She had
22	A heart—how shall I say?—too soon made glad,
23	Too easily impressed; she liked whate'er
24	She looked on, and her looks went everywhere.
25	Sir, 'twas all one! My favor at her breast,
26	The dropping of the daylight in the West,

27 The bough of cherries some officious fool
28 Broke in the orchard for her, the white mule
29 She rode with round the terrace—all and each
30 Would draw from her alike the approving speech,
31 Or blush, at least. She thanked men,—good! but thanked
32 Somehow—I know not how—as if she ranked
33 My gift of a nine-hundred-years-old name
34 With anybody's gift. Who'd stoop to blame
35 This sort of trifling? Even had you skill
36 In speech—(which I have not)—to make your will
37 Quite clear to such an one, and say, "Just this
38 Or that in you disgusts me; here you miss,
39 Or there exceed the mark"—and if she let
40 Herself be lessoned so, nor plainly set
41 Her wits to yours, forsooth, and made excuse,
42 —E'en then would be some stooping; and I choose
43 Never to stoop. Oh sir, she smiled, no doubt
44 Whene'er I passed her; but who passed without
45 Much the same smile? This grew, I gave commands;
46 Then all smiles stopped together. There she stands
47 As if alive. Will't please you rise? We'll meet
48 The company below, then. I repeat,
49 The Count your master's known munificence
50 Is ample warrant that no just pretence
51 Of mine for dowry will be disallowed;
52 Though his fair daughter's self, as I avowed
53 At starting, is my object. Nay, we'll go
54 Together down, sir. Notice Neptune, though,
55 Taming a sea-horse, thought a rarity,
56 Which Claus of Innsbruck cast in bronze for me!

I

WHAT so many commentators on Robert Browning's *My Last Duchess* seem not to account for is the form of the poem as a complement to, and a vital adjunct of, its intent. The work is not a narrative in limbo, one offered from the point of view of an omniscient poet with a particular pronouncement or moral lesson to aver and justify, but a statement of one hypothetical persona to another, a dramatic monologue—that "consists of three constituent parts: the occasion, the speaker, and the hearer." [1] *My Last Duchess* differs from, for example, *Soliloquy of the Spanish Cloister* or *Porphyria's Lover* insofar as in it one speaks directly to an identifiable other, both have demonstrable personalities, and the two are in a specific and detailed setting, the essential features of which seem completely comprehensible by the words of the one to the other. The 'monologue' aspect of the poem differentiates it from a soliloquy since, although the words of the poem emanate entirely from one of the personae, all are heard—and intended to be heard—by his immediate auditor. The poem, rather than being a narrative, is 'dramatic' because the whole of it appears to have been excerpted from the body of a play, of many characters and scenes and a conceivable plot; all of these dramatic features comprise the remainder, what precedes and what follows, which defines a drama of the reader's imagination, evocative but unwritten.

B. W. Fuson defined what he termed a "psychodramatic

---

[1] See Appendix D for notes.

1

monolog" as *"an isolated and satisfactorily self-contained poem successfully simulating a spoken utterance by a specific and subtly delineated individual clearly not the poet, uttered on a specified occasion and involving a particular localized dramatic situation of perceptible tensity, usually directed toward an individualized and responsive auditor, and affording the reader rich opportunities for insight into the speaker's personality."* [2]

Many of Browning's dramatic monologues, wrote Hiram Corson, are "a double picture—one direct, the other reflected, and the reflected one is as distinct as the direct." [3]

"The work of Browning," observed Claud Howard, "was the final perfection of the monologue, brought about by infusing the dramatic spirit into the old form of lyric origin; the dramatic monologue came to be a hybrid of two types of poetry, the lyric and the drama. The distinctive qualities of this form justify its classification as a new type—*genre*—of poetry." [4]

Chapter 4, "The Solitary Voice," of Park Honan's *Browning's Characters,* contains a thorough discussion of the dramatic monologue and its poetic problems and possibilities. Honan noted the many terms other commentators have given the form, many of which are highly illuminating—for example, "soliloquies of the spirit," "pseudodialogues," "a dialogue in which we hear only the chief speaker's part," "a dramatic scene in the history of a soul," "monodrama," "a drama of the interior," "subjective drama," "introspective and retrospective drama," "one end of a conversation," "a monopolized conversation," "a combination of discourse, conversation, argument, soliloquy, reminiscence," "a self-disclosure in which we have the collaboration of an analyst at work." [5]

"In the dramatic monologue," noted W. H. Griffin and H. C. Minchin, "so freely used in the shorter pieces of *Bells and Pomegranates,* Browning had hit upon the poetic form which was henceforth to be peculiarly his own. No unessential details are admitted, and the effect is commonly won by concentration and a sparing use of ornament. It is impossible to dissociate these merits from his experience as a writer for the stage and his observation of theatrical exigencies. . . ." [6]

But Browning's employment of the form of the dramatic monologue, as Fuson pointed out, was scarcely unique nor in particular innovative: ". . . Browning contributed virtually no technical innovation to his genre; in fact, it may be said to have been established a generation before his first dramatic monologs appeared in 1836. Far from being the inventor of the form, or even a pioneer in its external mechanics, Browning took over a ready-made vehicle used by scores of preceding and contemporary poets. Paradoxically as it may sound, Browning's better monologs actually exhibit a comparative restraint in the exploitation of the melodramatic potentialities of the genre; it was chiefly a more complex and brilliant psychography permeating the lines of his monologic poems that made them appear unique." [7]

Browning "is the successor of our great dramatists," wrote W. J. Alexander; "and no English poet since Shakespeare has seized and presented views of human life and character with such variety and vividness." [8]

Further, ". . . in the monologue Browning merely accepted a not uncommon form as an instrument for painting individual character more accurately than was possible in the sequent study of a single soul or the conversation of a contrasted group. As soon as Browning had created the Dramatic Lyric he abandoned play-writing altogether. The new method preserved all that was valuable both in it and its lumbering predecessor, attained the full individualism at which Romanticism had long unsuccessfully aimed, introduced a new type into English poetry, and brought before its readers such a company of living men and women as it had not seen since Chaucer died." [9]

"Essentially the Dramatic Lyric is a poem spoken by a person who is not the poet, but who is a person imagined by the poet and presented by him in a particular set of circumstances. As the speaker speaks his poem, his utterances express the effects of the impact on him of the given environment, situation, or circumstance." [10] "The monologue enables Browning to present his characters with an unusual directness. They are not described at one remove. They reveal themselves under the stimulus of some exceptional circumstance or propitious moment." [11]

But the form of the dramatic monologue contains enormous complexities in characterization, and even so straightforward a statement as John Bryson's wants some qualification: "In Browning's monologues every detail of the setting tells, and his tiny stage is peopled with fully rounded figures though only the main character has the speaking part." [12] That view, however praiseworthy it might be intended to be, could be considered inaccurate. To be "fully rounded" is neither actual nor necessarily worthy as an ideal; such people who are, said Robert Frost, can only roll. Neither Oedipus nor Captain Ahab nor Lear nor Milton's Satan is balanced and knowable; all are reductions of irrelevancy and expansions of whatever in us is vital beyond ourselves. In terms of Browning's dramatic monologues, the speakers purposely lack any semblance of rotundity in their personalities because most of his speakers confront listeners (and, often enough, readers) who could be expected to oppose the views they pronounce, and most are struggling against more potent forces to justify the actions they have taken or would take: Andrea del Sarto against his vicious and vacuous wife and his debilitating love for her, Fra Lippo Lippi against the artistic and spiritual limitations of those in power (who include the guardsmen, of "gullet's-gripe" and empty hats), the Bishop of St. Praxed's against the avarice of his "nephews-sons" who can see good reason for "no more *lapis* to delight the world!" In *My Last Duchess* the Duke confronts less a commoner, a man whom he could expect to approve the Duchess' behavior and disapprove the Duke's, than the fearful mirror of his own 'nobility' and the strictures of his own pain. The Duke, asserted C. N. Wenger, "is marked by internal discords and use[s] monologue utterance to regulate action that promises to solve [his] difficulties." [13]

For quite other reasons, Wenger denied any 'balance' in Browning's speakers or their listeners:

"Nowhere among the Browning delineations are there any full and rounded portraits, any viable personalities or completely analyzed character types. His personages lack integration with their environments and integration within themselves, too, both of which are essential for the realization either of complete character roles or of fully rounded personalities. Nevertheless, when appraised by apt criteria their limited portraiture is found to have a unique validity, for it pictures just those psychic phenomena which are ordinarily neglected or obscured in full delineations. Its excellence lies in its interpretive exhibition of those aberrations of the psyche which regularly flourish in any society, actual or fictional, during the collapse of traditional values." [14] In his essay Wenger calls for the need for psychoanalytic examination of the poet, who "used the dramatic monologue as an unconsciously assumed mask whereby to give his subconscious conflicts an outlet, or meditative release, which his conventional, optimistic acceptance of the old order would not otherwise permit." [15] Wenger would probably have included the Duke of Ferrara as one of the "dramatis personae of the nineteenth century who are beset with various psychic disruptions generally current in the decaying social order." [16]

The personalities of the other figures of Browning's dramatic monologues, other actions and conversations, other locations—all can be, with reasons justifiable by the immediate contexts of the immediate poems, hypothesized by the reader—or, rather, Browning's listener, for *My Last Duchess,* and his other mighty Renaissance monologues (*The Bishop Orders His Tomb at St. Praxed's Church, Fra Lippo Lippi,* and *Andrea del Sarto*) must, for reasons that should become apparent, be heard—or even seen with a perceptive mind's eye.

While not directly involving the action indicated *in* the poem, a short play has been written by Leila Wade that pertains to sundry antecedent actions. Unfortunately, the value of this play lies wholly in its (quite unintended) hilarity. The action of the work has somehow gotten confused with *The Ring and the Book,* and the murdered Pompilia's son Gaetano has wandered amorously into the life of the Duchess of Ferrara, to have such unperishing exchanges with her as:

DUCHESS (smiling, reaching out her hand for the fruit ["a bough of cherries"]): For me, Gaetano? Did you break them for me?

GAETANO (expressively): From the very heart of the orchard, for you.[17]

Gaetano, by the way, "is eighteen, rather mature for his years, yet with an engaging boyishness of demeanor. He is dark, eager, and extremely handsome."[18] In trenchant dramatic contrast, "The *Duke* is forty years old. He is tall, with a haughty carriage of the head and shoulders, which makes him seem even taller than he really is. His eyes are cold and searching. His face would appear impassive were it not for the look of extreme pride which is its habitual expression."[19]

The *Duke* enters with *"Frà Pandolf,"* who "proceeds to adjust his easel, and to mix his paints," and offer: "I can finish the portrait today if this light holds. . . . That is good, but my lady's mantle laps over her wrist too much. . . . I could paint the cherries more easily. Paint must never hope to reproduce the faint half flush that dies along the throat." At this, "The *Duchess* blushes, but makes no comment."[20]

All must end tragically, however. The *Duchess* is compelled to emulate the end of Socrates; *Gaetano,* "with a gesture of infinite grief," emulates Sohrab over the body of Rustum; and "The *Duke* is seen on the walk at the back, surveying the scene apparently without emotion, as he moves toward the right. The stage is darkened, gradually, completely."[21] The whole has only a bit less grace, depth, complexity, and subtlety than Eliza and the bloodhounds.

A drama involving the action implied in the work itself, in terms of staging and other speaking roles, has yet to be written, although in its mere fifty-six lines Browning has offered in the poem all except the complete dramatic form. Almost all requisite dramatic elements are present, the monologue wanting only a physical audience. Scrupulously enjoining the dramatist's art, Browning himself does not seem to project any moral strictures or judicial interference of his own beliefs; he allows his characters to convey their own personalities and the justification for their own behavior. Remarked one early commentator, "How he delights to work and worm and wind his way to the subtlest places of the soul, and to the maze of problems which the soul is perpetually seeking to solve! . . . He is a dramatist in all that we usually imply by that word, entering into the innermost arena of the being. His poems are, to quote the title of one of his dramas, 'soul tragedies.' . . . they present an order of tragedy different from Shakespeare's—the agony, the strife, the internal stress are more internalised. He transfers the circumstances of our being from the *without* to the *within*. In this way they all become noble pictures of the striving and attaining soul." [22]

However, Henry Jones, although not writing directly about the dramatic monologues of Browning, found the poet generally yielding to rather stringent moral strictures that antecede the works and pervade them, to their objective detriment: ". . . his moral interests are too obtrusive, and . . . he is too conscious of a mission, and a mission destroys the drama." [23] ". . . Browning found one theme whose interest was supreme, and . . . the subject which was all in all to him was not purely artistic, but also ethical" [24] "I find everywhere the poet's own mood and passion; moods and passions which have their root in some moral conviction, and which envelop the agents, subtly removing them from the ordinary life and giving to them an air of unreality and untruth." [25] Jones compared Browning as a dramatist to Shakespeare, and found the Master quite the opposite: "Of no one of Shakespeare's personages can we say, 'There is the author himself;' of scarcely one of Browning's can we say, 'There the author is not found.' " [26] Indeed, it seems not the least important and distinguishing aspect of Shakespeare's genius that he does not obtrude himself, does not take sides, but rather allows human passions and the inherent drama of circumstances to "spin the plot." *Shakespeare* never 'said' anything—Lear did, or Edmund or Goneril; Hamlet did, or Claudius; Othello did, or Iago.

"Fate often seems to hang by a thread," continued Jones; "and the pettiest incident may serve to set free the hidden forces in a character which otherwise might have lain dormant. The greater the dramatist, the better he knows this, giving outward circumstances their place without making his personages puppets. So the true dramatist is an observer and recorder and nothing more. He neither approves nor disapproves, but without either prejudice or partiality lets the characters evolve their own destiny in the outer world. This is the root of the magnificent objectivity of Shakespeare. This is why we cannot find him in any of his works. He has no preconceived theory, no dominant scheme of life, no likes or dislikes, but his bosom is broad as Nature's, and he sheds his sunshine on all alike. In a word, he gives them life and a world to work in, and then he stands aside while they pass judgment upon themselves." [27]

Quite to the contrary, "The defect in Browning's dramas is . . . not that they have unity of purpose, but that this unity is separable from the rest, capable of being defined; it obtrudes itself; it is aggressive rather than pervasive." [28]

Browning can be Shakespearean in certain regards, offered another critic, but he is no Shakespeare. "A certain dramatic understanding of the person speaking, which implies a certain dramatic sympathy with him, is not only the essential condition, but the final cause of the whole species. . . . Like the Shakespeare of proven knowledge in his throng of creatures, [Browning] can habitually merge himself in this man or that; and like the Shakespeare of conjecture in Sonnets, he can on occasion deliver his own soul; but he does not impress one as exceptionally able to see life steadily and see it whole, as Shakespeare does in the scope and implications of his greater masterpieces. He loves to break the white light through the medium of his own or a borrowed ego, and seldom reaches finality, except in so far as clear insight into truth in one of its aspects means implicit perception in the rest." [29]

Another commentator who would seem to have agreed with the appraisals of Jones and M. W. MacCallum is P. S. Grant:

"The art of Browning in monologue was developed, it would seem, as a consequence of moral qualities in himself and his time. He shared the serious questions of his generation, and desired to teach his fellows truths of the spirit. He chose a poetic form, monologue, because that form permitted a combination of action and description, where his personal interpretation of the story might at any time intrude itself. This method led naturally to a cold, metaphysical, and lifeless treatment of his subjects, which were little more than abstractions, until the discovery of Italy as a rich storehouse of personages and incidents fortunately rescued him, and gave his themes warmth and motion. Browning is never truly a dramatic poet,—one who lets life act itself freely before his readers. He muses upon life in every vigorous speech, to be sure, but still in terms of the intellectual rather than in terms of action. He is analytical, searching the consciousness of his characters for motives, moods, and spiritual processes, and these he expounds with all the virile brilliancy of his strong nature and the egoism of the monologue." [30]

The presence of such moral obtrusion and an inappropriate "intellectualism" that might debilitate the self-determination of his characters might well have considerable validity in regard to a number of Browning's works; yet, if such is the rule, *My*

Last Duchess (and, one would hasten to add, *The Bishop Orders His Tomb at St. Praxed's Church*) might appear to be the exception. The vast bulk of commentary on the poem has been written to remark, or at least to point up, the surpassing villainy of the Duke (see below); Browning, in such commentary, must a priori find himself in moral opposition to such a man. But the poet might have been here far more astute than many of those who find this small drama defective, for he makes the Duke— or, perhaps more accurately, permits the Duke to make himself —not wholly unattractive. Like Claudius in *Hamlet* and Edmund in *King Lear,* the Duke of Ferrara speaks magnificent poetry; and, though his "wit" be "witchcraft," that "wit" has nobility and pungency. Perhaps by making him the target of their hatred, the commentators have tacitly acknowledged his realism and believability; the greatest compliment that can be paid Browning in regard to *My Last Duchess* is that the Duke is a Shakespearean figure.

Another observer found Browning "so sympathetic with the poor girl's [the Duchess'] lack of aristocratic discrimination that he regards the Duke's mere recital of the story as sufficiently explicit condemnation of him. This little masterpiece is, I believe, the only dramatic monologue in which an enemy of Browning's gospel is allowed to speak for himself without heavily underscoring his own error or being exposed by a giveaway." [31]

But perhaps that "condemnation" is not quite so "sufficiently explicit," no matter how much of "an enemy of Browning's gospel" the Duke might be. In terms of this poem alone, that "gospel" would be rather difficult for one to delineate, much less extrapolate; and the patent eloquence, dignity, and extraordinary subtlety-beneath-subtlety of the Duke would not seem to be characteristic of a man who is being "condemned."

Wenger remarked that "During the first half of [Browning's] career a majority of his dramatis personae were of ages other than his own. In delineating them, he usually stood somewhat aloof from their inner conflicts, balanced the subjective and objective forces, and so managed to achieve many vivid portraits." [32]

G. H. Palmer, too, citing *My Last Duchess* (as well as *The Bishop Orders His Tomb at St. Praxed's Church* and *Andrea del Sarto*) as "illustrative" of "Browning's power as a constructive artist," eschews any moral intrusion or "preaching" on the poet's part—such as in *Abt Vogler* and *Rabbi ben Ezra*.[33] "Browning's Duke, displaying the picture of his last Duchess, is himself a full-length portrait. His dignity, courtesy, cruelty, interest in sculpture, in painting, unite, unconsciously and without exaggeration, to show this cross-section of a Renaissance aristocrat. As Browning's aim too is not moral instruction but the dispassionate study of individual character, good and evil qualities are allowed to intertwine in the same perplexing fashion as in actual life." [34]

It might well be offered, then, that in *My Last Duchess* "the author is not found." The "vividness" of the "portrait" of the poem is that of a man who "subjectively" might be "an enemy of Browning's gospel" but who "objectively" is a fascinating man, who, despite the limitations of the action of the poem (a man with large public responsibilities would understand more than such a man's ambassador), states his own case with eloquence and perhaps more reasonableness than most would seem to credit him.

If the present study can be said to have a purpose beyond an explication of the text of the poem, that purpose might be to view the Duke as an extremely complex man in a rather intricate situation—which is somewhat more involved than an overtly, even defiantly, villainous martinet being "explicitly condemned."

II

T HE Duke of Ferrara alone speaks in this poem—to justify his own actions, to arrange for a marriage, to exhibit his art treasures. Whether he might be considered on balance an evil or a pitiable man, Browning allows him to tell his own story in his own manner; and he evinces himself to be, at the least, enormously interesting.

An often-cited comment on the poem is that by Robert Langbaum, who, although he found the Duke "an unmitigated villain" and even called into question his "sanity," [35] remarked upon the man's "immense attractiveness":

"The utter outrageousness of the duke's behavior makes condemnation the least interesting response, certainly not the response that can account for the poem's success. What interests us more than the duke's wickedness is his immense attractiveness. His conviction of matchless superiority, his intelligence and bland amorality, his poise, his taste for art, his manners— high-handed manners that break the ordinary rules and assert the duke's superiority when he is being most solicitous . . .; these qualities overwhelm the envoy. . . . The reader is no less overwhelmed. We suspend moral judgment because we prefer to participate in the duke's power and freedom, in his hard core of character fiercely loyal to itself. Moral judgment is in fact important as the thing to be suspended, as a measure of the price we pay for the privilege of appreciating to the full this extraordinary man." [36] Langbaum attributed this seeming paradox to Browning's delight "in making a case for the apparently immoral position; and the dramatic monologue, since it requires sympathy for the speaker as a condition of reading the poem, is an excellent vehicle for the 'impossible' case." [37]

This 'danger' was underscored by William Cadbury, who would warn the reader about sympathizing with the "inhuman" Duke: "If the character's perverse attitude is too compelling, we may lose our bearings, forget the poet who controls the creature, and so read as final what must be only intermediate, a step on the way to philosophic thought." [38] It would seem that an 'obtrusive morality' is being forced upon the poet to curb what perhaps a reader would see as a "perverse attitude." Sympathy for the Duke, Cadbury wrote, is "absurd." "We must test the poem against our outside knowledge of what kinds of character Browning will create and how he will judge them, if we are even to begin to resolve the possible ironies. We must supply, from outside knowledge, awareness of the poet displaying his narrator and to make the effort to disrupt our reading of the poem." [39]

But such "character[s] Browning will create" include a wryly humorous old bishop who loves beauty and learning and passion more than he cares about the salvation of his own soul—which salvation, like the ornate trivia about his deathbed, is "vanity"; and an artist who "chooses" to "pay [his] fancy" in loving a worthless but beautiful bitch rather than seek immortality. It is, perhaps, not a "disruption" of "our reading of" *My Last Duchess* that would be desirable so much as a "disruption" of our own moral parochialism and ignorance of the power and purpose of art.

George Bernard Shaw, in the "Tragedy, Not Melodrama" section of his "Preface" to *Saint Joan,* regarded tragedy as devoid of villains, as consisting of opposing forces or elements or persons both of which have some justification for their actions, both of which—to a degree—are right. In *My Last Duchess*—and in this consideration it is not unlike a tiny *King*

Lear or *Antigone*—the two opposing forces, an imperious Duke with national obligations and a gentle Duchess with unrestrained appreciation, both harbor some right, perhaps in nearly equal degree, or some wrong, born of misunderstanding, also in equal degree. The result is not so much a moral horror story of virtue punished and vice rewarded, but a tragedy—without villains. And as in *King Lear* and *Antigone,* all forces lose. It is "a dirge over a marriage that was no marriage, but the death of two souls, . . . in the tragic implications of *My Last Duchess.*" [40]

The dramatic monologue, "since it requires sympathy for the speaker," seems to equalize the opposition and allow the reader to view the case for the side his own 'morality' would find objectionable or evil. The effect of the poem, after the settling of the dust of the cherry bough and the "nine-hundred-years-old name," is one of Thomas Hardy's "satires of circumstance," and a tragedy no less.

Browning's 1838 trip to Italy is fairly well documented,[41] and did not include Ferrara, which "in 1840 . . . had become the scene of half" of *Sordello,* his most ambitious poem to that time,[42] not to mention *My Last Duchess. Sordello,* Griffin and Minchin noted, turns upon an event that "has . . . no foundation in fact. . . . Now, except that Browning was dealing with real people and places, and—somewhat freely—with historical events, this story is as fictitious as that of Aladdin. . . . The real Sordello, also, was quite unconnected with Ferrara: he did not die there, nor did he die at the age of thirty: he is said to have lived to nearly three times that age." [43]

Griffin and Minchin mentioned that Browning "consulted" the *Parva Chronica Ferrariensis* in the British Museum, but only in much later life actually visited the city itself.[44] He might have seen pictures of the gigantic moated Castello Estense, home of the great Este family, and certainly knew something of that famous family's history (see Appendix A), but in *My Last Duchess* absolute historical accuracy is of little significant ac-

count either poetically or artistically. The histories of the particular individuals who might have been the rough basis for
the poem—Alfonso II, the Count of Tyrol (Ferdinand I or
Maximilian II), the emissary of the court of Tyrol to the court
of Ferrara, the unfortunate Lucrezia de' Medici—need not be of
overweening concern here. None in this poem appears by such
a title, designation, or name. Indeed, some strong doubt might
be cast on the efficacy of our knowing a good deal about their
biographical circumstances—or so much of the public 'events'
of a person's life as another can discover or be said to 'know.'
Browning has here not offered an account of events that can
be corroborated by historical evidence; he has created the characters in the poem rather than simply reflected other personages; and the encumbrance of one's learning, for example, that
the emissary might have been one Nikolaus Madruz might more
delimit than expand his willingness to accept the situation the
poet offers. He is the artist, the ultimate author; the persona of
the Duke mirrors the vital center of his own attitudes, although
his immediate words and actions are the poet's creation—the
essence of a lifetime of a human being compended into a short,
a very short, poem.

It is at least partly owing to that brevity and incredible com-
pactness that the poem has achieved such celebrity. Even more
often than this dramatic monologue is mis- (or under-) inter-
preted, it seems to be the object of unqualified admiration; for
example:

"Suggestion overpowers description. It's a gem for a royal
collection. Its value lies in the dramatic situation, the vivid description and the concentration of power. It's a work of the
imagination. . . ." [45]

" 'The Last Duchess' [sic] has the attributes of perfection,
lacking that certain undue insistence, and the sense of striving
after a colloquial diction, that largely vitiates the achievement
of [Browning's] dramatic soliloquies. The dialogue is unforced,
dramatic, and functional in a poetic way." [46]

". . . a miracle of compression." [47]

". . . that masterpiece of poetic concision, where a whole tragedy is burned in upon the brain in fifty-six lines. . . ." [48]

"What a wonderful portrayal in fifty-six lines! Many a long novel does not say so much, nor give such insight into human beings. Many a play does not reveal processes so deep, so profound as this." [49]

"*My Last Duchess* encompasses a novel in about sixty lines, a sense of the infinite complexity of life, of the under and overtones of existence. . . ." [50]

"The poem is a subtle study in the jealousy of egoism, not a study so much as a creation; and it places before us, as if bitten in by the etcher's acid, a typical autocrat of the Renaissance, with his serene self-composure of selfishness, quiet, uncompromising cruelty, and genuine devotion to art. The scene and the actors in this little Italian drama stand out before us with the most natural clearness; there is some telling touch in every line, an infinitude of cunningly careless details, instinct with suggestion, and an appearance through it all of simple artless ease, such as only the very finest art can give." [51]

III

THE very title of *My Last Duchess* seems less a label, a means of designation, than it does an additional source of the magnificent complexities of the poem and of its primary persona. It seems to be an extrapoetic commentary, perhaps the only one, by Browning on the Duke of Ferrara—the poet's word to us as readers about the man whom the poet, ultimately, allows to describe the situation and himself. The title of the poem is not merely a reflection of the Duke's first few words. The tightness of control habitually practiced by Browning appears to preclude any coincidence or casualness in the *"My"* commencing the work, the "That's *my* last Duchess" opening the speaker's words, and the "for me!" that completes them both, work and words. We are confronting one whose egotism must impress even himself.

The title should be pronounced with the emphasis on the middle word, since, from the point of view of the persona (and the consciousness of the poet), such is the principal subject of his statement (and monologue); "Duchess" could in itself refer to any possible previous consort, or consorts, or, indeed, to the subsequent one. The "Last" means the former or the latest, the most recent, of perhaps a rather lengthy succession. Nothing in the words of the Duke might be taken to indicate that his "Last Duchess" was either his only former consort or the latest of a number of former consorts—except that word "Last," which might suggest more a comparative than an exclusive designation, as would 'Late.' The Duke's history of marriages, of course, would be known to the Count, and to his envoy, so there would seem to be no reason why the Duke might wish to conceal the existence of any previous marriage(s); considering the present betrothal negotiations, however, there would seem equally no reason why he might want to call attention to them. It seems more tradition—and historical 'interference'—than contextual evidence that regards the "Last" Duchess as having been the only Duchess to the time of the Duke's monologue.

It is not to pass without notice that the term Browning employed is not 'Former' or 'Late' or another somewhat closer to denoting the woman's individuality. The poet, perhaps sardonically, perhaps more knowingly, reflects the woman as, ultimately, more a public "Duchess" to the Duke of Ferrara that she might have been a private 'wife' to Alfonso;[52] the term, in the Duke's words (lines 1 and 15), seems an appropriate referent for the Duke's auditor. But, of course, he does not speak the title: in his own eyes, there is no poem, no drama, but only his words to the Count's emissary. The whole is a 'poem' from the consciousness of the poet (and reader) alone: the title is Browning's, and from his at least partially caustic coign of vantage, it is *his,* the Duke's, "Duchess," a unique and especially animated possession, but royal property nonetheless.

It might help our comprehension of the work were we to consider ourselves a theater audience actually witnessing only the action onstage. We must assume, as two characters appear before us, that they have come from somewhere else. What occurred in the wings, left and right, or onstage before the curtain goes up or after it goes down, can remain only conjectural, to be hypothesized from the words that we hear when the two characters are before us.

The Duke of Ferrara and the emissary, or ambassador, or envoy, of the "Count" have apparently been closeted in a private sitting room on an upper storey of the colossal ducal palace.[53] The "company" (line 48) is "below." It would seem unlikely,

in particular consideration of the imperious nature of the Duke
—a trait probably not unknown to the emissary's "master"—
that this emissary would have bargained with the Duke about
the size of the "dowry" to accompany the Count's "fair daughter's self." Far more likely, the man has the task of closely
observing the Duke and, if possible, being able to return to
the Count with some notice of the Duke's financial expectations.
He appears not to have been able to secure such a figure, however, since the Duke appears never to have stated any (see lines
49–51). Putatively, then, negotiation was not the overt subject
of the upstairs conversation; that was elegant temporization
and obfuscation by a man who well knows that he is being tented
to the quick, and by his observer, who knows that the other
knows of his scrutiny. With grand offhandedness, the Duke
might have alluded to the "known munificence" of "The Count
your master" by appearing cognizant of some of the latter's important possessions, or the favorable circumstances of the Tyrol's
political position, or the Count's expansive holdings, or the like.
But it would seem that such information as the Duke has, has
been by means of his own envoys. He does not know the Count
any more than he knows his "fair daughter," so that *known
munificence* becomes a general comment, a diplomatic compliment that contains as much admonition and courteous,
courtly intimidation as graciousness. The emissary was doubtless
the man who had the less to say: not only is he not being employed to talk overmuch, but the fragment of ducal pronouncements that we, the audience-readers, are permitted to overhear
well enough indicates that the royal personage is accustomed
to his own monologues and rarely enough must have dealings
with another of commensurate stature. What transpired upstairs, then, when the two were cloistered, was probably elegant,
suave, most "skill"-ful "speech" about no demonstrable subject
matter at all. The Duke had, perhaps, with equivalent subtlety
and firmness, indicated to the ambassador his expectations for
the *next* Duchess—expectations underscored in the context of

the words of the poem themselves. Dowry, finances, expected behavior, the Duke's aristocratic prominence—all were communicated to the ambassador without a syllable spoken about any of them directly.

The two men have completed their elegant persiflage upstairs, and are on their stately passage through the long corridor and down the enormous staircase to "meet/The company below." That "company" would consist largely of sophisticated liegemen, factotums, and myrmidons of the Duke of Ferrara, who have been dutifully entertaining the train of the Count's ambassador. If the Count himself had come, lesser dukes, minor princes of state and church, and the like would have comprised that group of worthies "below." An ambassador would have to be content with the presence of the Duke's lesser relatives, the local administrators of the territory, and perhaps merely a bishop.

It would seem likely that, as the two proceed along that corridor and down that staircase, the ambassador a respectful, ambassadorial step behind his royal host, the latter has been pointing out some artistic treasures of his patrimony—perhaps not only those for the acquisition of which he has been personally responsible, although the two "pieces" he mentions in context were done during his reign, for *him*.[54] Well he knows what he is about, and he has a multiple purpose in indicating those treasures: he is preparing to talk about his "last Duchess" thereby, he is alluding to his wealth and nobility, and he is emphasizing his impeccable taste. Many of the works would be ancestral portraits—perhaps including one of a former ex-Duchess. Here, he might have semicondescendingly allowed, is a portrait of his great-grandfather Ercole I, or of his granduncle Ippolito I, Cardinale d'Este, or of his grandaunt Isabella, Marchessa di Mantova, or of his mother, La Duchessa Renea di Francia; here is a Tiziano, or Palma Vecchio, or Salviati, Mantegna, Parmigianino, Dosso Dossi, or a Lorenzo di Credi. He walks slowly, graciously bored amid the opulence and perfect taste of his splendid family. The portraits and other works extend the length of the hall and onto the wall bordering the staircase. That staircase must have been enormous to have supported a landing of a size sufficient to hold a divan—although not a particularly, and typically, sybaritic one—and some feet of viewing space before the portrait of the "last" Duchess of Ferrara. As the two men reach that landing, the Duke pauses. Of course, the ambassador, who most likely had been feigning a polite interest in the art, the artists, or the subjects of the works, stops also. He follows the Duke's gaze to an object he certainly has noticed before, as they began their descent, or a while before, as they went upstairs to converse. The object is a large, three-quarter-length portrait, strangely obscured, for the most part, by curtains hung from a rod affixed to the frame.

B. N. Pipes, Jr., argued that the work is al fresco, that the Duke's statement that the likeness of the Duchess is "painted on the wall" is to be read literally.[55] However, for various contextual as well as extracontextual reasons, the work would appear rather an oil, or a tempera and oleo-resin colors, canvas. In context, Browning is indicating, through the Duke, that it is about a portrait that the royal personage speaks; the "painted on the wall" would be, then, essentially expository, for the purposes of the reader's—not the ambassador's—comprehension. Were the phrase not included in the poem, the Duke's referent, here at the beginning of the poem, would be uncertain. In much the same manner, the Duke's identification of "Neptune . . . Taming a sea-horse," "in bronze," is actually gratuitous to his immediate auditor, since the latter quite well can recognize by his customary trident the Earth-Shaker, can recognize the action depicted in the work and the medium of its composition. In the tradition of the great Classical and Elizabethan playwrights, Browning here interweaves exposition of background information for the enlightenment of his audience and the words of the drama with a minimum—or a total absence—of external stage directions (see Appendix B).

But this portrait differs from the others in that it is nearly wholly concealed by dark curtains, no doubt of velvet or silk. The curtains are dark not only the better to 'obscure' the work, but because the portrait they almost 'conceal' is of one probably recently deceased.

That the painting is a *ritratto* is obvious: the curtains are not quite shut; and others, "strangers" to the palazzo like the emissary and therefore unfamiliar with this particular work, have "read"

> . . . that pictured countenance
> The depth and passion of its earnest glance,

and have looked to the Duke in deferential puzzlement as though to remark on the excellence of the work or the splendid features of its subject. Probably no one has ever "durst" to inquire, and probably the emissary has not "turn[ed] and ask[ed] thus." But were the painting entirely covered to present a would-be viewer with only the opaqueness of its total concealment, that "earnest glance" could never have been noted—and less, "read." There might be a brief and questioning look, but no one would "turn" or "ask," since no one would "durst" inquire into something that His Grace had chosen to secrete. But the Duke manifestly wants questioning, searching glances; he has apparently left a narrow strip in the center of the painting exposed precisely to elicit "strangers' " inquisitively "turning" to him. He wants almost desperately to talk about the picture— or its subject. He has had the portrait placed on the wall of the landing, an ideal location for contemplative, though not intimate, viewing. A divan has been placed on the landing to front the picture, much as galleries have divans, benches, or chairs opposite their most valued or popular works. It would seem to be a divan rather than a single chair fronting this painting because a chair certainly would invite the observation that single viewing is intended, which observation might lead to the further one that the Duke often enough views the portrait alone, unaccompanied, and hence that the subject is a manifestly vital one to him. Admitting tacitly to that would be to the Duke tantamount to acknowledging a personal disturbance, or even "stooping." Contrarily, divans spaced along the corridors to afford comfortable viewing places would in no manner seem at all remarkable. It would then be a reasonable surmise that the Duke not infrequently does regard this portrait by himself, from the comparative safety of a divan that can theoretically accommodate several simultaneous viewers, that the work in particular fascinates him, and ultimately that the subject—and not its possible aesthetic worth alone (see the last three lines of the poem)—moves or disturbs him. That anyone would deduce that the "last Duchess" strongly affects the Duke of Ferrara would indicate a weakness in him, an uncertainty, a hesitancy, a diminution of his assumed perfection; such notice would be for the Duke intolerable. For these reasons this particular divan would not be so attractive, comfortable, inviting as most of the others more typical of the setting of the palazzo.

Therefore a divan, a *cassapanca*—and Renaissance furniture, especially that belonging to so elevated a nobleman, was massive; therefore, the landing was enormous, the staircase enormous, the residence of the Duke of Ferrara a colossal palazzo, the setting of the poem grand, awesome.[56] In a visual regard alone, then, the poem's audience confronts a tremendous prospect.

One can be reasonably certain that the Duke would notice the ambassador's gaze even though the latter is behind him, or even were the ambassador suavely to attempt to conceal it, or were he, remarkably enough, not at all to take note of the curtained work. The Duke, it would seem, has left exposed the primary features of the face, or one eye, the "glance." He has in fact hidden little by the curtains but the rest of the subject's human form—itself scarcely unique—and the background of the subject, which we may assume is not of especial distinction of design even though fine in execution and totally appropriate to that subject.

One commentator believed that the Duke "had Frà Pandolph [*sic*] surround the Duchess with testimonials to her appreciation of the simple and naturally beautiful: a sunset, a bough of cherries, a white mule. She valued the Duke's favor—the painter has clearly given it first place among the accessories—but she did not value the artificialities within his castle. It was no accident that Frà Pandolph painted her clear of those walls which could have become nothing but a prison for her." [57]

Since the Duke is the patron and sponsor of the artist, however, it would seem most unlikely that he would request—or permit—a background depicting such items, "testimonials," as those he demonstrably abhors. Furthermore, her being painted "clear of those [castle] walls" because she "did not value the artificialities" they contained seems quite at variance with her liking "Whate'er she looked on," which would include the Duke, the "mule," the "favor," the sunset, the treasures of the palace quite as well as those of "orchard," "terrace," and beyond. Indeed, one of the Duke's major condemnations of the lady is that there was nothing that she did not "value." Pipes appears to have been accurate enough, however, in pointing out that, besides the Duke's "favor," the three items the nobleman mentions as sources of her delight are all characteristic of the outdoors; and the Duke does seem the indoor type.

Walking with "strangers" to the palace, the Duke does desire to notice their interest in the work, or even in the phenomenon of the partially closed curtains over it; the Duke wants to talk about the Duchess, perhaps largely to justify what transpired to her, and why, after a few preliminary, albeit purposive, remarks about the work as a painting, and the painting as a work of a famed artist. What he wants physically to conceal is the Duchess' portrait when he is not present. Exposing her is the equivalent of exposing himself as one who could not master her. She is gone now; and that mastery, never realized while she lived, asserts itself by his manipulation of a cord that draws curtains—scarcely satisfying control, but one that must suffice him now.

A large part of his consciousness knows that she has finally beaten him by making him recognize something about himself it would be better for him not to have known, and the frustration—even rage—beneath his ducal restraint must be terrible.

IV

THE two men walk slowly down the corridor. 'That *Crocifissione* is by Iacopo Bellini; that's my grandfather's sister Isabella, painted by Mantegna. . . .' They reach the great staircase and begin descending it. 'That's Dosso's portrait of Ercole I, and Oriolo's portrait of Ercole's brother Lionello, and,' he goes on with finely studied torpidity, 'that's my father, Ercole II, a Tiziano. . . .' They reach the landing. The Duke takes due note of the emissary's almost unavoidable gaze, pauses before the curtained work, and perhaps with a barely audible sigh of tolerant resignation, swiftly and decisively pulls the cord; with a softly rising metallic hiss, the sombre, heavy hangings part; and after looking at the painting for a moment and considering —again—the substance of what he will say, and brooding for a moment at the pain the portrait always gives him, the Duke turns slowly, regally, to the Count's emissary, and speaks, lending the opening (and later, the closing) of the poem the quality of an ellipsis, the drama's commencing *in medias res*. The curtains of the small play open for the audience simultaneously:

> That's my last Duchess painted on the wall,
> Looking as if she were alive.

He looks at the ambassador then, and not back to the portrait until he says "and there she stands" (line 4). Then he turns to the other man to speak, until " 'twas not/Her husband's presence only . . ." (lines 13–14), following which he takes little formal note of his auditor—other than lines 21–23 and 42–43, and the aside about his want of eloquence (lines 35–36)—until "Will't please you rise?" (line 47).

The Duke's immediate purpose in speaking about the painting—a purpose certainly not wasted upon such a shrewd and subtle man as this silent emissary must have been—is to communicate to him how this "last Duchess" fell far short of the Duke's expectations of how a Duchess of Ferrara must comport herself. Comprehending, then, how she failed in her regard of the Duke and his ancient patrimony, the emissary will carry his impression back to his "master," who would thereupon warn his "daughter" of what might well befall her were she to be so unselective in her valuation of the many "gifts" that would be visited upon her. Such is the Duke's immediate rationale in speaking of his "last Duchess" to the emissary, and he has most carefully plotted what he will say, if not the actual words; he has enough confidence in his articulateness to preclude a rehearsal of his "speech."

Laurence Perrine enumerated three "motives" for the Duke's speaking as he does to the emissary: "He wishes (1) to stipulate politely but clearly what he expects for his share in the bargain, both as to dowry and as to daughter, (2) to impress the envoy with his position, his power, and his importance, and (3) to flatter the envoy so as to ensure a favorable report on the envoy's return to his master. He accomplishes all three purposes." [58]

The curtain has lifted; the actors have entered the stage of our immediate perception. The Duke indicates by a nod the barely revealed—or, rather, barely concealed—portrait, and speaks. The "painted on the wall" appears to indicate that he is close enough to the painting just to have opened the curtains in front of it; the more distant, affectedly uninvolved "That" refers more to the subject than it does to the painting. "Looking as if she were alive," addressed directly to his listener, would seem to reflect the appearance of the work to another, a verbal reflection of what such a "stranger" might be thinking. Since the two men have been discussing, after their own diplomatic indirection, the preliminary arrangements for the proposed union with the Count's "fair daughter," the nobleman's use of the word *"Duchess"* need not appear strained or in any way a compromise of the context in which they had been conversing; indeed, that would appear to have been the only reasonable, consistent referent for the woman. However, the term certainly does connote an enforced distance; he does not seem to think of her as his former 'wife,' in her private, or body natural, regard, but as the woman who for a time contributed the assumed services of the necessary female sharer of the title, a consort, a Duchess —pure body politic. What the Duke intends by "last" probably is *former; latest* does not appear to be a term to be employed before a man who would, perforce, represent the interests of the *next* or *newest* one—a designation hardly promising for the lady's well-being, longevity, and good fortune. By "Looking as if she were alive" the Duke indicates to the ambassador verbally what the curtains manifestly symbolize, that the lady is dead, and not the possibility that she might now be in a nunnery or otherwise dispossessed of both her title and "husband"; the Duke, at the outset of his remarks about the lady, wants to communicate that her death is a certainty.

"I call/*That* piece a wonder, now" [59] does not indicate the Duke's not being near enough to the painting as yet fully to expose it; the term used is "That," which rather evidences both his possessive regard of the "piece" rather than its subject, and a continuation of his apparent emotional remoteness from the subject herself—or so he would have his listener believe. The "last Duchess" is offered for the moment, and here to the emissary, as a portrait, a work of art, as the bronze of Neptune and the sea-horse will later be offered; the figure is a "piece" of superb craftsmanship, a treasure, itself a "rarity"; it is an object that might be "a wonder," but more so aesthetically than personally. Apparently at one time, perhaps during the Duchess' sittings, the Duke of Ferrara, "connoisseur to his fingertips"

that he is supposed to be,[60] considered the work somewhat the
less to be valued, because he does amend, after the slightest of
pauses, "now," the reason for his former hesitation in pronounc-
ing it "a wonder" following the colon:

> Frà Pandolf's hands
> Worked busily a day, and there she stands.

T. J. Assad asked whether "the painting seems all the more
lifelike now that the Duchess is the 'last' Duchess. Or is it that
the Duke has learned something about art?" [61] Neither of those
two possibilities seems sufficient to account for the "now," the
first because the Duke must see himself as admiring the work
rather than its subject, the second because he would scarcely
acknowledge to another that his judgment of art has ever been
less than that of an exemplar.

It might seem an extremely subtle petard that hoists the Duke
here, but Stanton Millet believed it could be one nonetheless,
and one peculiarly his own. Millet's thesis is that in the Duke's
considering the portrait "a wonder" because it portrays the
Duchess as being deeper and better than one could credit her
with being in life, he has ignored what might well have been
in the lady all along:

"As the Duke fully understands, the question [of "How such
a glance came there"] stimulated by this intriguing glance involves not only the relationship between the portrait and the
living woman, but certain conscious or unconscious assumptions
about that relationship. In asking 'How such a glance came
there,' the strangers and the envoy show that they take the portrait to be a reflection of the Duchess' total personality, of her
reaction to some specific circumstance, or of both at once. They
further reveal that they do not consider the portrait an end in
itself: they assume (since they are, significantly, strangers who
do not know her) that the living Duchess was more interesting
and perhaps even more complex than her portrait suggests.
Having anticipated this question, the Duke had begun in his

first remarks to the envoy to expound what he apparently considers a remarkable irony: there was nothing in the situation nor in the living Duchess' personality to correspond to the complexity of her painted expression. He mentioned Frà Pandolf because the painter was solely responsible for whatever is of interest in the Duchess' expression. That is why he considers the portrait 'a wonder.' "

The Duke's "primary, conscious motive is to explain the contrast between the portrait and the living model. To argue that he denounces the Duchess *because* of 'the depth and passion of her earnest glance' is to obscure the richest irony of his lecture. He is able to maintain his tone of chillingly casual objectivity because he is convinced that the living Duchess was quite unlike the portrait. . . . As for her 'earnest glance' in the portrait, that too was Frà Pandolf's work: the living Duchess, he insists, was a fatuously good natured woman who smiled at everyone who passed. She missed and exceeded 'the mark' in so many ways that the Duke found her, as he says, disgusting.

". . . While we cannot know the portrait except in the Duke's description of it, we can legitimately ask whether it is a 'good' or a 'bad' likeness on the same grounds that we ask about the true nature of the Duchess. That is, has Frà Pandolf given the admirably ingenuous Duchess a conventional 'depth and passion'? Or has he perceived in her a depth which was really there but which the Duke was unaware of?

". . . If it is indeed a true likeness [since it "satisfies Fra Lippo Lippi's requirements in that it reveals both beauty and soul"], the Duchess escapes the Duke in the painting as she escapes the charge of his indictment. Her real depth of soul, caught in the portrait, is revealed to everyone but the Duke, and he, admiring the painting for its expression [as "a wonder" of the painter's art] but failing to see that art in this instance truly reflects reality, is again convicted of tastelessness and lack of discrimination." [62]

In other words, the "piece" is "a wonder" to the Duke because

it is such an accomplished artistic portrayal of an undistin-
guished subject. But to anyone else except the Duke who might
have known her, the "piece" would be, rather, an accurate
transfer of that "deep and passionate" lady to canvas, the "earnest glance" that was ever an inseparable part of her preserved
quite undiminished or altered. The portrait, then, is rather the
truth than "a wonder."

The Duke wishes to project the idea—which quite possibly
he himself believes—that the famous painter "Frà Pandolf"
was all in a flurry of eagerness obviously to please His Grace
alone; the painter differs from other "officious fools," who have
the same objective, by being talented—even, as the Duke will
mention in a moment, celebrated for his excellence. *He* not only
"Worked busily a day," but his "hands" did, effecting the image
to the Duke, thence to the ambassador, that the man was in a
terrific agitation to please his royal patron. The quickness with
which the words pass seems to complement the rather derisive
images of the servile painter the Duke wishes to project: "busily
a day" depicts the painter's ostensible zeal to complete his work,
subsuming his artistry, if necessary, to the Duke's demand for
a finished portrait.

The duration of the painter's efforts is quite often taken to
mean one day, or no more than a few hours of sitting.[63] But
"busily a day" might more imply "busily" "day" after "day"
(after "day"). With heavily stressed syllables before and after it,
"a" seems to be barely audible, distinguishable as a separate
word, as the Duke speaks; 'one' would seem a more germane
word were he either stating or intimating that "Frà Pandolf"
did his work within that brief span. If the portrait is on canvas,
as it appears to be (see Appendix B), its completion in several
hours, *one* "day," is unlikely from at least two major considera-
tions: portraits painted in the Renaissance generally occupied
the artist two to three weeks or longer—and even the extremely
few fresco portraits took at least a week for completion;[64] and
the Duke of Ferrara's wanting an extremely hasty work would

be most inconsistent with, even antipodean to, both his familial pride and the superior artistic sensibilities that he believes he has.

The Duke avers that "Frà Pandolf's hands," note, did not paint; they "worked": even as a painter he remains a worker, almost a laborer, for the Duke, just as the renowned "Claus of Innsbruck" is later mentioned to have "cast in bronze"—a figure again more of menial than of creative effort—another "piece" for the Duke.

> . . . and there she stands,

the nobleman pronounces rather perfunctorily.

V

Turning back to the emissary, the Duke as much as commands him to be seated upon the convenient divan, and not so much to "look" as listen: "Will't please you sit and look at her?" "Her" in this line expresses both the subject of the portrait and a hint of the Duke's subsequent discourse; it does not seem to be about the painting itself, then, that he wishes to speak. He wants to talk about his recent Duchess and then does so by way of the expedient of talking about her portrait—initially, about the making of her portrait. But the elegance—or, depending upon one's current view, the pomposity—of the man causes him to phrase the injunction in as politic a manner as he can, rendering it urbanely interrogative (see also line 47). The divan has been placed on the landing opposite the painting the better for one to view it, but the Duke alone "puts by/ The curtain," so that he manifestly wants to speak about the work—or, rather, its subject—not infrequently. He has a specific, external, demonstrable purpose for doing so now; but the surmise is that there might be another purpose, more subtle and immediate to his own self. ". . . look at her," he tells the emissary; listen to her, learn about her, learn from her, learn about me from what I shall tell you of her, he means.

The contiguity of the "she" (line 4) and "her" (line 5) seems a quick transition from the subject of the painting as the sitter of the artist to the subject of the painting as a personality to the one speaking. Perhaps the Duke noticed the "her" after he

37

had said it and, lest his auditor think, however briefly, that the Duke is more concerned, at least at this point, with the woman than with a "pictured countenance," the Duke at once speaks of "Frà Pandolf" (see Appendix C).

As though to anticipate the emissary's idea that perhaps the Duke insists too much on the authorship of the portrait, and also to keep the subject of the painting herself away from him a little while longer (thereby building the anticipation he feels in talking about the lady), the Duke mentions the painter again, indicating that he well recognizes the intent of his own words. "I [did say] 'Frà Pandolf' by design," he avers; I say everything "by design," he intimates; I have not committed even the veriest of errors; I do not make mistakes.

One rather bizarre, not to say forced, explanation of "by design" was offered by N. B. Crowell: "Her naive acceptance of the obvious flattery of Frà Pandolf, who calls the blush to her cheeks as much for perverse sexual pleasure as for art, is hardly to be construed as a revelation of the poverty of her intellect. Perhaps she was aware of the imperious decree of her husband that the painter finish the portrait in a single day as a means of occupying hands suspected of dexterity in the art of love as well as of painting. If this surmise is correct, her blush might be appropriate to a much more worldly woman than she is." [65]

And E. E. Zamwalt would have the Duke himself, because he is "ignorant of Christian virtues," hint that the portrait "reveal[s] sexual implications which indict the Fra and the Duchess. Loveless and jealous, he thus completely misunderstands and condemns the general spirit of love and courtesy, the basic assumptions of Christian love, which the priest and the Duchess differently symbolize." [66]

But almost all the critics who have chosen to comment on the subject agree that the Duke's "design" was rather to obviate this extraordinary possibility of a liaison between the Duchess and the painter. P. E. Kilburn, for example, believed that the emphasis in line 6 ought to be on the first word, " 'Frà,' " because thereby the Duke rejects the idea that "that depth and passion seem to compromise [him] by implying that the painter had been her lover, for no such glance would ever come on the face of a woman not in the presence of her lover. Yet the name 'Fra Pandolf' itself explains and refutes the implication. . . . The Duke assumes that his audience will know that the Fra's vows are good. The fact that Pandolf is a monk is refutation enough of the implication of the Duchess' glance." [67]

The Duke's "use of the name 'Frà Pandolf,' " wrote Assad, "is clear evidence that he is purposely minimizing the role of the artist. The 'Frà' may indeed be meant to indicate there was no 'affair' between the Duchess and the painter. . . ." [68]

L. S. Friedland wrote that "Perhaps it is not too fantastic to imagine that Browning made his Pandolf a 'Frà' to remove all wrongful implications of an 'affair' between painter and Duchess," [69] and "Not even the Duke, her husband, suspects her of wrong-doing." [70] And Leonard Burrows observed that "Part of [the Duke's] intention [in speaking of her], no doubt, is to make it quite plain that his late wife's 'depth and passion' did not blot his 'scutcheon with anything so positive and shameful as conjugal infidelity—he has not been cuckolded." [71] "The Duke's indictment of his last Duchess starts from that earnest glance of depth and passion depicted by Frà Pandolf, whose name is mentioned 'by design'—presumably to disabuse the onlooker of any suspicion that the glance was called forth by the personal charms of the artist." [72]

And Alexander wrote that "so full of self-revelation and feeling was the expression [in the Duchess' portrait], that a stranger might suspect some tender relation between sitter and painter; the husband, therefore, names the artist Frà Pandolf, whose well-known character would preclude any such suspicion. . . ." [73]

There is nothing in the poem that might even remotely suggest that the Duke had cause for a mistrust of the Duchess for any illicit involvement, and it might seem that many commentators bring up the point in order to dismiss it. No more guilt would fall upon "Frà Pandolf" than would attach to the "white mule" (which, just as rationally, might have been "mentioned" instead of a "horse") by an accusation—or an accusation by a denial of that accusation—of the Duchess for the tendencies of Catherine the Great. Sexual implications in this poem are not justified by the context; even a hint of a possibility of a sexual relationship between "Frà Pandolf" and the Duchess is poetically and artistically grotesque.

"By design" the Duke mentions the painter because His Grace wishes to boast of his patronage; he wishes to justify that patronage by spreading the artist's name; he wishes to evidence his own taste by indicating that no other artist could so excellently freeze the essence of the Duchess (or what it ought to have been), could so perfectly "picture" in a portrait her (idealized) "countenance" in life; and, as Browning himself responded when asked "By what design?", the Duke wishes "To have some occasion for telling the story, and illustrating part of it." [74]

Further, Renaissance painters who were friars were scarcely the rule, but not so uncommon to warrant especial emphasis on the "Frà" title of "Pandolf"; Browning readers ought to know of Frà Lippo Lippi, Frà Angelico, Frà Lorenzo Monaco, and perhaps also of Frà Bartolomeo della Porta. And Matthew Pilkington readers (among whom was Browning) might know, in addition, of Frà Simone da Carnuli, Frà Tiburzio Baldini, Frà Paolo Pistoiese, Frà Agostino Leonardo, and so on.[75]

In his time, "Frà Pandolf" either did have considerable celebrity or the Duke is trying to establish it by mentioning his name—three times in sixteen lines—perhaps to justify his own patronage of that portraitist. But the painting indeed must have been an exceptional one, and other visitors might very well have wished to ask its owner about the subject or identity of the artist ("if they durst"). But the ambassador probably never did ask—although one critic would have had him ask aloud, in so many words, about the painting, "How such a glance came there," after the first four lines of the poem, or "immediately after he has been invited to 'sit and look at her.' " [76] However well such a question by the ambassador might serve the plot of the poem, it would appear adventitious to the Duke's words, such a question could well be incorporated into his most active and potent silence, and it would be dysfunctional to Browning's technique—and genius—in the dramatic monologue. Andrea del Sarto's wife smiles a few times, turns her head, cocks her ear, rises in anger, and perhaps even takes the key he offers to open a drawer in order to get "the thirteen scudi for the ruff" —but she says not a word. Lippo's and the Bishop of St. Praxed's audiences are similarly active; but because a monologue is a monologue, no one but the speakers speaks a word.

The leisurely and solemn lecture and the frigid formality and imperiousness of the Duke of Ferrara, and the oddity of the drawn curtains not quite covering a painting in an obvious position to be examined, the normal diplomatic deference— all perhaps contributed to the ambassador's curiosity and puzzlement; but such curiosity would infrequently be expressed before this Duke. What the ambassador quite probably did was to note the curtains (from a considerable distance, or as the two men walked up that staircase an hour or two before), to glance at the Duke in order possibly to elicit an explanation, and to regard, almost clandestinely, such features of the subject as one could distinguish through the slight opening. Of course, the Duke would note the direction of the other's gaze, even had that been only marginally perceptible. One might appreciate the Duke's notice as the two men went upstairs for their private conversation and his restraint in preserving this coup for nearly the last impression he wishes to make upon the ambassador. He had, perhaps, alluded to his "last Duchess" before, without granting any specific information or reflection to an emissary a significant aspect of whose mission was to discover the reason for Ferrara's current marital availability. His earnest interest and concern have patently been whetted, and he does look to the Duke with that interest, of course understated in the direction and sharpness of his gaze: he himself must be an awfully suave and subtle man. He "turn[ed]" with his head and shoulder, he "ask[ed]" with a slightly raised eyebrow; but his political and ambassadorial position would seem to proscribe one word of overt concern. If the Duke chose to speak of, or ignore, one of his innumerable possessions, he would do so; he would not be persuaded or dissuaded by another. So much the emissary must already have learned.

The latter does as he is bidden and sits on the divan—not quite comfortably: to relax would have been a most inappropriate liberty. The Duke of Ferrara stands to one side of the parted curtains and addresses him:

> I said
> "Frà Pandolf" by design, for never read
> Strangers like you that pictured countenance,
> The depth and passion of its earnest glance,
> But to myself they turned (since none puts by
> The curtain I have drawn for you, but I)
> And seemed as they would ask me, if they durst,
> How such a glance came there; so, not the first
> Are you to turn and ask thus.

The iambic pentameter simulates speech, and speech is ordinarily prose, so that this eight-line segment actually simulates one 'sentence'—a magnificent burst of articulateness (as are lines 48–53) that expresses ideas rather difficult to utter. "Frà Pandolf" alone among artists now, the Duke posits, has such skill to transfer to canvas that "depth and passion of [one's] earnest glance." (The word "its" rather rawly, defiantly, renders the subject of the painting as neuter; here the Duke somewhat compensates for his use of "her" [line 5] when he wants to speak more of the painting itself than about its subject.) Any "stranger" would "seem" to "ask me" with his own "earnest glance" about the heart of this remarkable woman, so extraordinarily frozen forever by the artist's skill. The Duke offers the emissary a vague compliment in wanting to note the latter's would-be question about the subject of the portrait and not alone regard his glance as a mark of mere curiosity about its bizarre concealment, the cause of other, less intelligent and appreciative, "strangers'" covert "glances," the Duke intimates; most of the "strangers" to the palazzo are just inquisitive, but some few—like you—"would ask" an intelligent question or two—"if they durst."

Manifestly, no one would be so cavalier (or, maybe, suicidal) as to open the curtains himself; indeed, no one would be so impolitic and presumptuous as even to inquire about this lady or "How" the portraitist worked his skills. The words by which the Duke describes the expected behavior of "strangers" are cautious and oblique—"seemed," "would ask," "if they durst." No one, he softly avers, would have such temerity. The parentheses of the Duke—those asides ever softer than soft—are devastating; they stiffen him, render him even more remote, unattainable, gray, gothic. They are supernally articulate.

> (since none puts by
> The curtains I have drawn for you, but I)

expresses in gentle monosyllables (save, of course, for the 'technical' word "curtains") a rather intricate statement. The jewels of that clarity are the verb "puts by" and the pause, indicated by a comma, before "but I"; "puts by" seems so rational, even automatic, natural, inevitable, that any other term would become a compromise of verbal proportion; and that pause so subtly underscores his incredulousness at anyone's even asking about this work "painted on the wall."

You "ask thus" with your politic eyebrow, offers the Duke; and that "asking" would be as overt, as manifest, as verbal, as the direct question that you—or anyone else—"would ask me" —"if they durst." Two "ask's," and not one word spoken by the other; yet he knows that he *has* "asked" with his glance and he cannot demur.[77]

The Duke certainly would not expect any questions regarding the painting, since such a breach of etiquette, a base and unconscionable disregard of *noblesse oblige,* is unimaginable. I am the Duke of Ferrara, he need but whisper; but his royalty might appear largely on the surface. "Frà Pandolf's hands/ Worked busily a day" for *me;* no one "durst" "ask" the Duke of Ferrara so intimate a question as one regarding the "pictured countenance" of the subject of any one of the many portraits in the vast palazzo; no one, indeed, would dare to address any question at all to him. He will say what he will say, and he will omit what he will omit. The almost inaudible 'ah' before and after "if they durst," and the strong emphasis on the verb further stress his imposed, and assumed—though, perhaps, not wholly *self*-imposed, and assumed—remoteness, detachment, and ducal elevation.

The Duke refers to the emissary on four separate occasions (lines 13, 26, 43, and 53) as "sir," quite possibly as further insistence upon his own comparative status: so important and regal a figure as he could not be expected to remember—perhaps even to have heard before and then forgotten—the name of so comparatively insignificant a man as an emissary, an envoy of another, a hired agent. Even acknowledging that the man indeed has a name, a separable personality, would be somewhat a compromise ("stooping"?). But the Duke is so condescendingly egalitarian and mockingly democratic (lines 53–54, obviously, mark the apotheosis of such an attitude), that he does call the other "sir"—an "eminently safe" designation in that, exteriorly, it seems in no wise even suggestive of condescension. And it does directly, with its sharp and arresting sound, and at least quasi-personally, with its overt politeness, involve the emissary; it does demand his close attention to the words and intonations of the Duke; it does even seem respectful.

He turns from a brief regard of the painting to the envoy now, quite purposefully, with that incisive, democratic, vilifying word. The other man hastily meets the speaker's eyes, then looks back to the Duchess as the Duke does so (line 16). He is learning rapidly when to observe the man, when the painting when the Duke's eyes are on it, and when deeper homage would be served by his gazing at the portrait before him as the Duke looks at him.

In a brief study that credits neither Browning nor the Duke, nor envoy nor reader, with any measure of intelligence or subtlety, Ethel Mayne tried to observe the words and implied action of the poem from the consciousness of the envoy; she equated his reactions to the Duke's monologue with what she expected the right-thinking reader's ought to be. The envoy, throughout the monologue, sits in "mute amazement and repulsion, listening to the Duke, looking at the Duchess." [78] He "listens, with a thought of his own, perhaps, for the next Duchess! . . . More and more raptly he gazes; his eyes are glued upon that 'pictured countenance' and still the peevish voice is sounding in his ear. . . . And almost he starts to hear the voice echo his own thought, but with so different a meaning—

> '. . . There she stands
> As if alive'

—the picture is a wonder!

"Still the visitor sits dumb. Was it from human lips that those words had just now sounded? *'Then all smiles stopped together'?"* [79]

When the Duke has finished saying what he wishes to say about the Duchess and has closed the curtains, "The envoy rises, but not shakes off that horror of repulsion. Somewhere, as he stands up and steps aside, a voice seems prating of 'the Count his master's known munificence,' of 'just pretence to dowry,' of the 'fair daughter's self' being nevertheless the object. . . . But in a hot resistless impulse, he turns off; one must remove one's self from such proximity. Same air shall not be breathed, nor same ground trod. . . . Still the voice pursues him, sharply a little now for his lack of due deference:

> '. . . Nay, we'll go
> Together down, sir,'

—and slowly (since a rupture must not be brought about by *him*) the envoy acquiesces. They begin to descend the staircase. But the visitor has no eyes for 'wonders' now—he has seen the wonder, has heard the horror. . . . His host is all unwitting. Strange, that the guest can pass these glories, but everybody is not a connoisseur. One of them, however, must be pointed out:

'. . . Notice Neptune, though,
Taming a sea-horse, thought a rarity,
Which Claus of Innsbruck cast in bronze for me.'

". . . Something else getting 'stopped'! The envoy looks." [80] Commensurate with the surface level of the politeness of the "Sir," "Her husband" as the Duke's reference to himself appears to play down his own importance, in a continuation of his mock humility; but the position of the qualifying "only" enforces its emphasis in pronunciation and well evidences that that humility might be protested a bit much. "Only" that "presence" of "Her husband" would be quite sufficient "For calling up that spot of joy" noticeable in the "pictured countenance," the Duke posits; but he now commences speaking as directly about her as a woman as about the subject of the portrait. "Pictured countenance" seems the transitional phrase, evocative of both portrait and Duchess. Perhaps as well, the word "husband" casually emphasized, shouted softly, does suggest that he was "only" that to *"her"*; this is the first indication in the Duke's monologue of her indiscretions and the root of her failure as his Duchess of Ferrara. She had confused his public, body politic, function with his private, body natural, character (but, then, so perhaps did he). His calling her "the Duchess" (line 15) might well underscore her indiscretion: she was ever to me my "Duchess"—*the* Duchess" of Ferrara—while I was for her "Her husband" *"only."* At the same time it should be noted that the Duke consistently refers to her as "the Duchess" and by the noncommittal "she" and "her," and not once as 'my wife.' His intent is unmistakable.

VI

SAVE for a comparatively few passages in his Italian poems of this period, Browning does not appear to have been concerned with the art of painting except in its evocation of personalities; and the bulk of *My Last Duchess* is involved with the Duke and the Duchess rather than with the portrait, save as it reveals them. Poses for Browning reflected attitudes, expressions reflected feelings—of the subject and perhaps of the artist in the work when created. The vast range of the Italian Renaissance lay open before him, but he chose for his poetry only those manifestations, qualities, appurtenances of it that seemed most meet to the personae and situations of his poems. The background of many of those poems is Northern Italy of *quattrocento* and *cinquecento* times, but the focuses are quite universal and ubiquitous: death, in *The Bishop Orders His Tomb at St. Praxed's Church*; personal artistic expression, in *Abt Vogler* and *Fra Lippo Lippi*; jealousy, in *Soliloquy of the Spanish Cloister*; integrity, in *Pictor Ignotus*; love, in the masterpiece, *Andrea del Sarto*; or pride, in *My Last Duchess*. The sublime, personally transcendent elements of, for example, Andrea del Sarto's or Frà Filippo Lippi's art remain distinctly subordinate to the poet's purposes in his poetry; it would seem that the historic Andrea and the historic Filippo Lippi scarcely matter. The mere "craftsmanship" ("low-pulsed, forthright") of the former and the 'naturalism' ("simple beauty and naught else") of the latter offer better, more humane, more vital and diagnostic stories than either the historical evidence of a critic's regard of art largely for its own sake.

G. K. Chesterton noted that "Browning's interest in art was in a living thing, the interest in a growing thing, the insatiable interest in how things are done. Every one who knows his admirable poems on painting—'Fra Lippo Lippi' and 'Andrea del Sarto' and 'Pictor Ignotus'—will remember how fully they deal with technicalities, how they are concerned with canvas, with oil, with a mess of colours. Sometimes they are so technical as to be mysterious to the casual reader. . . . These Browning poems do not merely deal with painting; they smell of paint. They are the works of a man to whom art is not what it is to so many of the non-professional lovers of art, a thing accomplished, a valley of bones: to him it is a field of crops continually growing in a busy and exciting silence.

". . . he made himself to a very considerable extent a technical expert in painting, a technical expert in sculpture, a technical expert in music.

". . . The love of Browning for Italian art, therefore, was anything but an antiquarian fancy; it was the love of a living thing." [81]

No matter how great his "love . . . for art" might have been, however, distortion for a purpose often enough outweighed accuracy. Whether that purpose justified that distortion is a matter rather too large for the scope of the present study. And it should be mentioned that Browning's interest in art as "living," "growing," and "insatiable" is far more characteristic of the more experienced man. Browning was but thirty years old when *My Last Duchess* was first published, and his passion for art itself, and that of which it is capable, doubtless "grew" as he became more mature.[82]

In a somewhat more involved and detailed analysis than Chesterton's, William Whitla observed that Browning was enmeshed in relating the Renaissance to his own times, by means of a study of painting, and "the aesthetic experience of art as art, and, more important to him, of art as life." [83] Whitla pointed out that Browning's Duke, although quite thoroughly involved with art, failed to correlate it to the life it depicted because of his "defect in respect to love." [84]

Edward Dowden similarly found in Browning's Duke the paradox of passion for art and insensitivity toward passionate humanity, represented by the Duchess' "inward breathings and beamings of the spirit. . . . Never was an agony hinted with more gentlemanly reserve. But the poem is remarkable chiefly as gathering up into a typical representative a whole phase of civilization. The Duke is Italian of Renaissance days; insensible in his egoistic pride to the beautiful humanity alive before him; yet a connoisseur of art to his fingertips; and after all a Duchess can be replaced, while the bronze of Claus of Innsbruck—but the glory of his possessions must not be pressed, as though his nine hundred years old name were not enough. The true gift of art—Browning in later poems frequently insists upon this— is not for the connoisseur or collector who rests in a material possession, but for the artist who, in the zeal of creation, presses through his own work to that unattainable beauty, that flying joy which exists beyond his grasp and for ever lures him forward." [85]

"*Personality*," noted Pearl Hofgrefe, is "the source of Browning's interest in the arts." [86] She pointed out that by 1855 (*Old Pictures in Florence*) he had considerable knowledge of Italian art, but in his previous works (*Pauline, Paracelsus, Sordello, Pippa Passes,* etc.) mention of paintings and sculpture is of little textual importance. "Browning's early trips to Italy (in 1838 and 1844) seem to have small influence on his poetic treatment of painting. . . ." [87] In despite of Chesterton's statements, Browning appears to have known the names of artists rather more thoroughly than their works or manners; and it is those names, some quite arcane, that appear in his poems, not studied observation of the works—which, most often, might not seem vital poetic (or humane) material. Thus, there are references to Correggio, Annibale Carracci, Tiziano, Giulio Romano, Giorgione, Niccolo Pisano, Guido Reni, Pietro di Cortona, Salvatore Rosa, Bazzi, Beccafumi, Canova, Primaticcio, and others scattered throughout his poetry, with little attempt at particularly close observation of any one of them. "The arts . . . he loved also," wrote Hofgrefe; "but he loved them most because they recorded human experience, and best when they most fully expressed the struggles of the soul, and thus became the direct embodiment of personality." [88]

But such views of art generally that Browning had might be most admirable in themselves, without direct regard to particular artists. Those views seem to depend on the observation of a work of art by one who is less concerned with complementing his own present than he is passionate always to replace that present with further knowledge, perception, insight. His artistic 'truth' is never static; *that* is "living," "growing," and "insatiable."

However, in the process of his various historical distortions, Browning has given us a superb case for considering the artist himself as the primary determiner of his own work, and, in *Andrea del Sarto* one of the cruelest, most extraordinary love poems ever conceived. And in *My Last Duchess* Browning phrases qualities of portraiture, he verbalizes the otherwise purely pictorial, as exactly and exquisitely as has ever been written. And the poet, with open magnanimity, allows his Duke so to verbalize:

> . . . called that spot
> Of joy into the Duchess' cheek . . .

and

> 'Paint
> Must never hope to reproduce the faint
> Half-flush that dies along her throat'. . . .

And with equal, even negligent, magnanimity it is the Duke who allows "Frà Pandolf" either to have uttered or to have suggested those words and those descriptions. Yet, this is a confusing poem at least partly through intentional ambiguity; it is a poem of *however's, seem's, perhaps's;* and it might quite well have been "Frà Pandolf" who indeed did utter those felicitous phrases. The Duke is immensely eloquent about his Duchess, but he avoids speaking, save in the most practical and functional and proprietary terms, about the portrait itself. The Duke himself does not evidence an especially profound knowledge of art; he speaks mostly about *her,* not the portrait. He might be less a "connoisseur" than merely a collector.

Much has been made of the Duke as an aesthete, though primarily to distinguish him from being merely a prideful but empty nobleman of no demonstrable virtue at all; indeed, most of those who must admit a grudging admiration for the man do so because of his supposed artistic acumen, but otherwise he stands guilty of decadence, of absolute and irremediable villainy. "It is only as Art that the Duke can accept the 'depth and passion.' Life is beyond him." [89] "The duke . . . treasured his last duchess simply as the source of a wondrous pictorial arrangement. . . ." [90] "The Duke is a man of considerable artistic perceptiveness. . . ." [91] ". . . the man . . . shows a certain fineness of intellect. The Duke is a critic by education, and has a delicate taste in matters of artistic judgment. . . ." [92] Langbaum wrote of the Duke's "taste for art," [93] and L. R. Stevens echoed him, adding that the Duke "has an unimpeachable sense of the fineness in things. . . . Like a connoisseur he delights in the delicious beauty of the artifact, and he drops names such as 'Frà Pandolf' as testaments to the rare quality of his taste." [94] "The Duke has given the emissary a lesson in art appreciation," wrote Assad, "and has illustrated the theory that the magic of art lies precisely in this: that by mere selection, isolation, and direct transference the artist can make striking and significant what in real life was considered commonplace and meaningless." [95]

One might take issue with all such ideas, and with what could be taken as their summary and rationale: ". . . the whole emphasis of the poem has been on the painting of the last duchess." [96] The Duke's pictorial descriptions—"The depth and passion of its earnest glance," "that spot/Of joy," " 'Paint/Must never hope to reproduce the faint/Half-flush that dies along her throat' "—could be taken as quotations from or paraphrases of "Frà Pandolf" that the Duke finds, but could not publicly allow (and certainly could not before his present auditor), to be attractive phrasing. His description of those aspects of the portrait that another, because of inferior artistic taste or perceptive abilities, could not see, is minimal. He calls it "a wonder, now," calls attention to its "deep and passionate" "glance," but otherwise only recounts its plot, as he irrelevantly—to the envoy—describes what Neptune is doing in the bronze sculpture.

His being a "type of material-minded collector" [97] who has a "callous dedication to collection" [98] might seem rather flippant remarks, but they could have considerable merit. The Duke has a passion for possession, and is justifiably pleased in the treasures of his royal House; but their worth for him appears to lie only in acquisition and ownership as aggrandizements to himself and his ancient "name." The genius of the artist in doing exactly what "Frà Pandolf" appears to have done—purging the irrelevant and merely transitory; creating a permanent truth from a kaleidoscopic pattern of momentary essence and continuous, reproducible, nongermane trivialities and mediocrity; making the ephemeral worth an immortal reduction of form, shade, color, attitude, of painting

> —The beauty and the wonder and the power,
> The shapes of things, their colors, lights and shades,
> Changes, surprises,—

—that genius might be out of the range of the Duke. It might be "Art" and not "Life" that is "beyond him." But he is, in this poem, lecturing on the lady and on himself, not about art, not about the portrait; and his intelligence in saying exactly what he intends is so considerable that he might not be wholly blind to what he had ordered to be "painted on the wall" and "cast in bronze." Again, one is reminded of the form of the poem, which directly involves the speaker's thorough awareness of the one to whom he is speaking; the envoy would not be a suitable audience for "a lesson in art appreciation." [99]

The Duke quotes "Frà Pandolf" rather carelessly: the Duke of Ferrara, just as he 'cannot' remember the envoy's name, also 'cannot' be bothered with recalling the "chance" remarks of a painter whose "hands/Worked busily a day"—"for me!" But he "perhaps" has remembered the words because of their reverence, submissiveness, deference, and—he would want to consider —their obsequiousness. Besides, he could not, and now cannot, be annoyed with such ducally conceived trivialities as *ars gratia artis*. If His Grace must be extemporaneous and casually bored, then "Frà Pandolf" would be somewhat less so, and that invariably pleased Duchess would have been enthralled by the artist's "courtesy"—"stuff," blatant flattery, to the Duke, gracious compliment to the Duchess. Both "perhaps" and "chanced" accentuate the Duke's low-voiced cursoriness about those remarks.

> perhaps
> Frà Pandolf chanced to say 'Her mantle laps
> Over my lady's wrist too much,' or 'Paint
> Must never hope to reproduce the faint
> Half-flush that dies along her throat' . . .

It would seem as though the painter is excusing what he might conceive of as the inexactitude of what ought to be considered an exceptional portrait; that it is exceptional even with "Frà Pandolf's" urban apologies attests to the Duke's insistence upon perfection—in himself, in the preservation of his ancient "name," in his property, in his Duchesses (past and to come). The "erring lace" of "my lady's" "mantle" is more delicate than dainty, more fine than precious. As if only to satisfy the Duke,

"Frà Pandolf" also demanded perfection. His 'excuses' sound like servility (to the Duke), but they seem eloquent as well; the words, the description, are elegant beyond measure. The words are *perdendosi;* they fade, soften, mellow, as does the "faint/ Half-flush that dies along her throat." The *f*-sounds emphasize the fading of both the shading in the portrait and the words that describe it. A paraphrase of those words could but crudely suffice; they themselves are pictorial. Browning does, "Frà Pandolf" might, the Duke perhaps could not emotionally afford to, understand. That glory, because he is "only" the Duke of Ferrara, must remain "such stuff" offered solely to please himself; ". . . she thought" it was "courtesy"—grace, tribute, sincere and spontaneous observation—"and cause enough/For calling up that spot of joy," [100] and she was happy and delighted; she "blushed" with gratitude, pleasure, ingenuous responsiveness. But also with undifferentiated, unaffected "joy," and that involuntary indiscretion sealed her doom.

The Duke, yet standing possessively, casually, regally beside the painting, glances at the ever-attentive emissary to speak the next few lines. He speaks slowly, deliberately, pausing between each monosyllabic word; the *h*'s cannot be pronounced anything but somewhat heavily.[101]

> She had
> A heart—how shall I say?—too soon made glad,
> Too easily impressed . . .

That "heart . . . too soon made glad" seems the apotheosis of the Duke's observation of his Duchess. Her innocence at taking "Frà Pandolf's" "courtesy" to the Duke—self-evident, expected, *pro forma* to him—as gracious homage to herself seems such abrasive indecorousness that the Duke affects pause and elegant difficulty in forming the words with which to formulate her. The "how shall I say?", preceded and followed by dashes to underscore his drop in voice and his most unaccustomed puzzlement, almost like *ritenuto* and *morendo* musical notation, is accompanied by a brief glance downward; her ingenuousness had been almost grotesque, quite without precedent to him. The iambic pentameter seems relatively heavy here—"had," "heart," "soon," "glad" carrying the weight of her personality for him. He expected an a priori restraint of her, a care only for her Duke and what he had given her in gracing her with the inimitable title of Duchess of Ferrara. What that restraint entailed did not include a "heart," if that word connotes love, indiscretion born of love, affectionate regard, cheerfulness, good humor; "soon" means, again for the Duke, cursory, innocent, fortuitous; "glad" implies accepting, indiscriminately pleased, generally responsive, appreciative, open. That general affection and undifferentiated sympathy, that "heart," was "Too easily impressed." His carefully rehearsed—or, merely, not altogether spontaneous—"too soon made glad," to be spoken *meno mosso,* brings upon the comparative *poco più mosso* of the counterpointed "Too easily impressed"; those words move quickly: his 'sudden inspiration' at having—after a space—so articulately summarized her "heart . . . too soon made glad" appears to stimulate the swiftness of "Too easily impressed." Those three words are singly contemning, and cumulatively censorious: no Duchess of Ferrara must be "too" anything—"soon" or "easily," "glad" or "impressed"; she must respond to nothing "easily," give or speak or view or accept nothing "easily" or "gladly"; and, above all, she must never be "impressed" by anything since she is to be continuously conscious of the item to which all other "gifts" must invariably be compared. Quite to the contrary, the Duke is averring, she was ignorant of whom he had made her, and by extension indifferent to him. These words are drawn out—"*Too e*asily impre*s*sed." It would seem a dense emissary indeed, not a man to be employed by the Count on such a delicate mission of both princely diplomacy and personal import, who does not understand exactly what the Duke is saying; for a few moments their cold eyes meet, before the Duke's gaze slowly returns to the painting.

> . . . she liked whate'er
> She looked on, and her looks went everywhere.

From another man in other circumstances, the words might seem a pellucid expression of love and appreciation and returned affection. Here, they are a condemnation, bitter in intent but typically soft, neutral, in tone. The description once more is almost visual, perhaps sufficiently so to preclude exemplification; but then, no hired ambassador, himself perhaps not awfully distant from being an "officious fool" in his "master's" employ, could be so subtle as the Duke. So the latter exemplifies. The reader, even with no portrait in oils or tempera before him, sees the lady in Browning's most articulate Duke's portrait in words, gestures, emphases, pauses. One envisions the living Duchess "liking"—smiling gently, "blushing," murmuring her gratitude to a beautiful world of kind people and wondrous objects—everything, "whate'er/She looked on"—"and," conjoining the inevitable perspective, there was no limitation of her purview; the next words—and the "and" renders them so—seem as inevitable as a Vivaldi conjoinder: "her looks went everywhere." That last word is long, as long as any the Duke speaks here, and he takes the full measure of its length; if the "whate'er" is shortened as much by understated scorn as by rhyming and metric expediency, the "everywhere" is literally just that: "her looks went e-ver-y-*where*."

VII

"**S**IR" is said sharply, with a quick look at his listener, so stilly seated in the slight physical discomfort the lesser man must always affect. Such an affectation must certainly have been perceived with approval by so subtle a Duke; of course, his continuing to speak in the same tone must remain his singular acknowledgment of the emissary's expected deference and responsiveness. The phrase, " 'twas all one!" seems the more to have been addressed to the portrait of the Duchess, the exclamation only a moderate one, the words themselves unexcited. He might seem almost pitiable here if his words—or, at least, their substance had not been so meticulously prepared. The "all" echoes the "whate'er," the "everywhere," the "too easily," the "too soon": they are inclusive, generalized words; there was seemingly no limit to the unfortunate woman's *lèse-majesté*. The pervasive monotony of Tennyson's Lotos-Land, "where all things always seemed the same," was for the Duke the same order of pervasive monotony as the Duchess' pleasure; the words might be as anguished as his public surface will permit him to utter, but they bear the terrible personal burden of what her behavior appeared to tell him: he was of no remarkable difference from a bouquet of flowers, or a sunset, or her gentle white mule; " 'twas all one!" to her.

With those words, one commentator has observed, "the Duke reveals only that the Duchess had but one smile for whatever pleased her—a husband or a mule. And well might the Duke be irritated, for his Duchess lacked that quality which Browning associated with true love: it is the matter and the manner of 'One Word More' in which he extols the beloved's keeping some hidden facet of herself for the exclusive enjoyment of her lover—the moon's other side, as it were, never seen by common earthlings. Whether or not the Duke deserves this kind of love is utterly irrelevant to the poem." [102]

There had been, ostensibly, no "hidden facet" of the Duchess reserved for the Duke or for anyone or anything apart from him; and in this regard she—although for quite different reasons—is like the easily accessible "moon" of Andrea del Sarto:

> . . . my moon, my everybody's moon,
> Which everybody looks on and calls his . . .

This burden demands an explanation, so the Duke offers especially irritating instances of that sameness, "one"-ness, undifferentiated awareness of relative importance to her. *She* never learned the efficacy of affecting the envoy's deferential discomfort, tone, averted eye, humble and attentive silence.

> . . . My favor at her breast,
> The dropping of the daylight in the West,
> The bough of cherries some officious fool
> Broke in the orchard for her, the white mule
> She rode with round the terrace . . .

That "favor at her breast" seems distinctly understated, a trifle such as are the other items the Duke cites as instances of her indiscriminate pleasure. It would have been a brooch, a cameo, necklace, superbly cut jewel, string of pearls—any of which had been in the Ferrara dynasty for a long while; he would have lent it her for the duration of her reign as his consort. Like her title—and his—it was revertable to the body politic of the House. Her gratitude for such a "favor" ought to have been unmistakable, reserved but genuine: it was, after all, a symbol of what it was that he had bestowed upon her,

against which all else becomes a bagatelle beneath regard, nothing—that ancient "name." The other examples of "whate'er/
She looked on" are mentioned by the Duke with increasing
contempt: the sunset, a careless bouquet of flowers, a "white
mule." "The dropping of the daylight in the West," the *di-
minuendo* of the sound an echo of the word's meaning, is a
constant occurrence, daily, and—for him, at least, as it seems
to most people (presumably including the envoy)—repetitious
—and, to be sure, one quite independent of the Duchy; and
that she "liked" as well as his "favor," and the great title itself.

The contempt the Duke has for that "officious fool" is wither-
ing: the latter is "some" because his individuality is beneath
notice, "officious" because he had the temerity to intrude his
nonentity upon the Duke, to become a temporary competitor
for the Duchess' attentions; and most of all he is a "fool" since
he must certainly have been attempting, by a most unsubtle
stratagem, to please the most approachable Duchess in order to
please the most unapproachable Duke. He is a "fool" to have
believed that he could even remotely cozen the Duke by his
manifest deceit. The alliterative "*officious fool*" accentuates
His Grace's contempt. The Duke could not believe in even the
possibility that such a minor functionary—for the Duke—was
also a human being who might have "broke in the orchard" a
"bough of cherries" for the Duchess because he liked her and
wished thereby to please her. Furthermore, "broke" is not the
equivalent of 'made up a bouquet of'; it seems so perfunctory
and casual, 'snapped off.' The Duke immediately perceived the
cheapness of this "gift" of "some officious fool," whereas she did
not, or could not; "broke" well illustrates that perhaps jaun-
diced perception of his. It has been noted that "the repeated
b's and the emphasized stress on 'broke' reflect the action of
breaking the bough, and, on a dramatic level, the anger of the
speaker." [103] Arthur Beatty noted the anacrusis of this line,
which certainly must be complementary to the angry "*Broke*,"
as well as the anacrusis beginning line 43 ("Never to stoop"),

which reinforces the Duke's determination never to demean himself.[104]

The "bough of cherries" had probably not been given her in his hard-eyed presence; instead, he might have found it in her chamber, noted its offhanded severing while she remarked on its beauty and the kindness of the man who had favored her by the offering.

The "bough," the sunset, the rides on her mule all seem rather nebulous, unfocused examples, yet they also could have been cited as cases in point of her indiscretion because they were sources of actual observation by the Duke; they might seem to be too arbitrary to be otherwise. One could see her standing with him on a "terrace" effusively admiring a sunset, or showing him the blossoms, or calling to him from muleback to remark upon the gentleness, the beauty, the accomplishment of her "white mule"; and one could hear her "approving speech" of thanks for small favors, or see her "blush" of gratitude "at least"—"that spot of joy" the Duke admires so much in the painting, detests so much in the woman. And one could observe the Duke's lips set in grimness and exasperation at her indiscretion and blatant want of knowledge of whom he had made her. One could discern the childlike ingenuousness of the Duchess, the growing blackness of the Duke.

>   —all and each
>   Would draw from her alike the approving speech,
>   Or blush, at least.

Perhaps the difference in the times she spoke or just "blush[ed]" came to be determined more by his proximity than by the nature of the objects she beheld; "at least" she might have learned only to "blush" and to try to contain her small exclamations of delight when she knew he was about. Somehow she vaguely sensed his displeasure, though she could never have fathomed a reason for it. Her indiscriminateness extended to "all" things and "each" thing; she never accepted anything—sycophancy, a

docile mule, even a peerless setting for twilight—as due her because she was the Duchess of Ferrara, because she never came
to understand the unique glory of that title, that which "her
husband" had given her that far more than outbalanced "all"
else.

The Duke, however, could never consider himself so petty
as to wish her to act ungraciously in acceptance of the per-
quisites of her title. It was "good!" that "she thanked men"
(though not sunsets or a "white mule"), so long as those thanks
were edged with the requisite disdain, framed by the nod of
patient indulgence of one accustomed to and therefore tolerant
of sycophants, "officious fools." No man could rebuke her for a
tone of indifference or slight boredom in a muted, urbanely
understated 'Thank you'; but such had not been her form.
Those four words—"She thanked men,—good!"—punctuated
as they are—seem to be spoken evenly, the "—good!" somewhat brusque, to convey 'expected,' 'accepted,' 'perhaps very
well the way she ought to have behaved.' Then the pace slows
as the Duke, in another "—how shall I say?—" calm before
dazzling eloquence, looks away as he forms the *mots justes:*

> . . . but thanked
> Somehow—I know not how—. . .

The second "thanked" appears stronger than the first, with a
suggestion of his disparagement, as he explains the "Somehow,"
with a tenor, a glimmer, an incipience of that "spot of joy."
That calm of words spoken with even a discomfort of explanation, those dashes and open syllables of "—I know not how—"
precede the storm of one of the most spectacular marriages of
metrics and words in all of poetry:

> . . . as if she ranked
> My gift of a nine-hundred-years-old name
> With anybody's gift.

The meter of the poem is generally iambic pentameter, that

form of poetry in English that most closely approximates actual speech; but such meter seems irregular as the Duke underscores certain words and syllables. Line 33 begins regularly enough— "Some*how*—I *know* not *how*—as *if*"—but then the irregularities commence: ". . . as *if*"—the words emphasizing the extremity of the Duchess' irresponsibility—"*she* ranked"—a trochee, stressing the first word, the temerity, the extreme bad form of one who had been nothing before her magnificent elevation—"*My* gift"—again a trochee, with the "*My*" counterpointing the "she," the contrast of "she" with her arbitrary and totally malinformed "ranking" with what I had presented her, "*My* gift." The second trochaic foot, moreover, has the effect of preparing the pyrrhic "of a" and increasing the number of unaccented syllables to three, the soft preceding the resonance, the pastel affording greater chromatic brilliance, to the triple spondee "nine-hundred-years-old name." Those words are clearly, sonorously articulated, emphasized, extended; and the antiquity becomes almost palpable; the "name" seems especially protracted. The ancient titles of Duke of Ferrara and Duchess of Ferrara become of an age that is staggering (see Appendix A). The hyphens render the antiquity even more linear than one or two or three millennia: it is a "nine-hundred-years-old name." It almost, but not quite, strains credulity; it seems at the limit of anyone's conceptualizing of the House's age. That is what he has given her.

And "she ranked" that "gift" of his "With anybody's gift." Those last three words, six syllables, are almost spat out with the Duke's contemptuous comparison; they comprise three quick iambs, the weight being on "*any-*"—on that "officious fool," that one "who passed" her eliciting "the same" response she gave to me (lines 44–45); and on "gift," since to her what *I* had given seemed no more than a "bough of cherries" or a pleasant ride "round the terrace" on her tractable "white mule." He faces the envoy, frowning, his incredulousness inviting the envoy's sympathy, his responsive incredulousness, almost his equal disgust. The genius of those lines leaves the reader almost breathless.

The Duke seems to pause here for a few seconds, on the level of the drama, to allow the enormity of the Duchess' indiscreetness sufficiently to impress itself upon his listener. When he does speak again, he asks the rhetorical

> Who'd stoop to blame
> This sort of trifling?

The "trifling" is what the Duchess—indeed, any noblewoman of large responsibilities—must know, the black-and-white distinction between "My gift" and "all and each" of "anybody's gift." So to explain the difference to her must be a "sort of trifling," far beneath the Duke of Ferrara to bother with even to censure, to rebuke, "to blame": so "to blame" would be to "stoop." Just as the Duchess—for her quondam "husband"— appears to be writ fine in her "heart . . . too soon made glad," so the essence of the Duke—again, as he regards himself—lies in his refusal to "stoop." He uses the word three times in speaking to the emissary, and the word acquires the force not so much of 'condescend' as 'compromise one's lofty position' by the admission that she is the source of sufficient disturbance to move him from an orbit that has been uncompromisingly regal; in like manner, the placement of a single chair fronting the painting on the staircase landing is "stooping," and (as will be discussed later) his having had her murdered is also a variety of "stooping." At any rate, Ferrara questions whether anyone at all could have explained to her her failure to recognize his matchless "gift"; that, for any husband to any wife, would seem "stooping," compromising a not wholly unreasonable pride in his being not alone a man or a "husband," but a Duke—moreover, the Duke of Ferrara. He continues by saying—asserting, insisting too much on his assertion, and thereby possibly even supplicating—that even were a man to explain to "such an one" (which phrase renders her rather coarse, common, and a

most ordinary woman) her shortcomings and to allow her no
argument, he could hardly have been expected to comply.

> Even had you skill
> In speech—(which I have not)—to make your will
> Quite clear to such an one, and say, 'Just this
> Or that in you disgusts me; here you miss
> Or there exceed the mark'—and if she let
> Herself be lessoned so, nor plainly set
> Her wits to yours, forsooth, and made excuse,
> —E'en then would be some stooping; and I choose
> Never to stoop.

Once more the Duke gently protests his eloquence by calling
the emissary's attention to his supposed want of it: ". . .—how
shall I say?—", "—I know not how—", and now

> . . . Even had you skill
> In speech—(which I have not)—. . .

The silent emissary must think (and that is, of course, part of
the general plan) the other indeed an eloquent man, who apolo-
gizes for inarticulateness and then offers most precise, astute
declamations; "His disclaimer of such skill is part of the evi
dence for it." [105]

However, the irony is rather strong that the Duke indeed did
not have enough "skill/In speech" to explain "to such an one"
her failings. That his diction and manner might just have been
too formal and elegant and his argument too abstract, hence
incomprehensible to her, would be clear. Even his possible
"commands" *to* her were beyond her intellectual range. Sometimes rather blandly simple injunctions are more effective as
an argument, but that "skill" the Duke did not have. He has
"skill/In speech to make [his] will/Quite clear to such an one"
as the emissary, and it is in *that* "skill" that he takes perhaps
justifiable pride. Contention, wrangling, quibbling, remonstrat-
ing—those are "skills" he disparages and is not displeased not
to be able to claim as his own.

Besides, truth to tell, the lady might not have been very bright. Assad termed her "phenomenally shallow," [106] and explained the impossibility of the Duke's—or anyone else's—teaching the Duchess anything at all: "He asserts that he was too proud to stoop to lessoning his Duchess; but of course the problem was insoluble: the idea of teaching an instinctive reaction is logically absurd." [107] And Margaret Bates's celebrated comment might be quoted in this context: "It was her perpetual smiling that provoked the Duke—smiling just the same for everything and everybody. . . . It was the deadly monotony that got on the man's nerves. What is more wearisome than a continual smile?" [108] One is reminded of Tennyson's comment about the miserably mismated Carlyles, cited by Chesterton: Tennyson "could not agree that the Carlyles ought never to have married, since if they had each married elsewhere there would have been four miserable people instead of two." [109]

Here, by disparaging "skill/In speech"—like "skill" in carving or "skill" in dancing or "skill" in knitting; trifles all—and so softly, with not alone dashes in this case but the *sub rosa* parentheses, the punctuational equivalent of the tilted head and the dissenting hand palm upward, the Duke diverts his listener before again astounding him with fantastic verbal agility and brilliant understatement.

"He is," as Perrine wrote, "at that very moment by indirection making his will most clear to the envoy as to what he expects of his next wife. The Duke is vain," he added, "but he is no fool." [110] The man does not 'speak in paragraphs,' but in dramatic monologues, in iambic pentameter, in rhymed couplets!

VIII

THOSE enjambed rhymed couplets in the poem, in regard to the speaker, serve as a complement to his articulateness by their relative casualness of intonation: the couplets themselves lend the impression of formality and tremendous verbal "skill," while the enjambment softens that formality to a tone more suitable to the Duke's auditor and the Duke's purpose in addressing him, while retaining that eloquence and "skill."

Quite to the contrary of A. A. Brockington's statement that "the verse form of the dramatic monologue does not matter," [111] the use of rhymed couplets in *My Last Duchess* contributes significantly to both the poem and the effect of the Duke's monologue; but such a contribution would not be only a technical achievement or merely the phenomenon of a *trompe d'oreille*, at which some commentators would leave it. Others are sometimes more circumspect:

"Whatever we may think of 'Sordello' in other respects, we must admit that it is a masterpiece of rhymed measure. The 'run-on' lines are so frequent that we hardly notice that they are arranged in heroic couplets. In Pope . . . there is a point and a pause at the end of nearly every line; here not one line in seven is thus marked off. A person not familiar with the poem might listen to long passages read with proper emphasis and expression, and take them for blank verse. The same is true of shorter poems in the same measure. Take, for example, at random a passage from 'My Last Duchess'. . . ." [112]

"The meter is interesting. It is the heroic couplet, the same form in which Pope wrote his major productions. Yet the rime, which is as evident as the recurring strokes of a tack-hammer in Pope, is scarcely heard at all in *My Last Duchess*. Its effect is so muffled, so concealed, that I venture to say that many who are quite familiar with the poem, could not declare offhand whether it were written in rime or blank verse. This technical trick is accomplished by what the French call overflow, the running on of the sense from one line to another. . . .

"One has only to glance at the printed page of *My Last Duchess*, and see how few of the lines end in punctuation points, to discover the method employed when a poet wishes to write a very strict measure in a very free manner." [113]

"Browning's pentameter couplets have two noteworthy characteristics: their openness and their comparative regularity. They are in no sense heroic couplets; they are distinguished from regular blank verse in nothing but rhyme. . . . The couplets are wide open. The thought lengthens out from one line into another until sixty per cent of the lines are enjambed. The rhymes are not only unobtrusive, but they frequently leave the reader quite unaware of their presence." [114]

(The presence of enjambment between couplets, or between the verses within a couplet, precludes those couplets' being called "heroic"; further, "heroic couplets" are primarily moralistic or aphoristic, whereas rhymed couplets are primarily narrative, descriptive, or conversational.)

"In the versification of *My Last Duchess*, the most marked feature is the great freedom of flow, combined with terseness of expression. It is in the rhyming couplet, but the rhyme does not obtrude itself, because of the use of enjambment in those lines where the thought demanded an unbroken flow. It reads like blank verse through most of the poem, until within a dozen lines of the end, when the rhyme comes out strongly, completing at once the sense and the effect of regularity and system in the structure of the verse." [115]

"Though the even flow of the verse in this poem is very noticeable, it will be found on examination to have no merely
mechanical regularity. As a whole, the verse of the poem is
calm and stately, in keeping with the proud, elusive character
of the speaker. But, when the thought and feeling demand it,
there are departures from the normal iambic flow, which are
most expressive." [116]

C. W. Smith noted that "Fantastically strict as they are, even
to the syllable count, perfectly rhymed, these couplets are so
manipulated rhythmically as to give the impression of dramatic
conversation. They have no small part in making the poem at
once memorable but in no sense does the traditional rigidity
of their form constrict the flow of action. For the reader they
produce a stimulating conflict between prescribed form and the
rhythm of dramatic speech." [117]

Two statements by Burrows further elucidate the poetically
complementary function of the verse form:

"The rhythms have the run of speech, but are retarded by
the formal couplet-rhymes across which the sense often easily
steps, but never rushes; the informal formality of the patterning
so lightly imposed on the flexible rhythms echoes the tone of
the Duke's confidences—'I choose to tell you this, my good sir,
but pray take no liberties.' " [118]

"Rhythms, syntax and diction have a conversational quality,
yet Browning has taken for his metrical form the rhymed iambic
pentameter couplet. It is decidedly the 'open' couplet that he
uses, and there are many 'run-on' lines since syntactical pauses
rarely coincide with couplet-endings or line-endings. The resulting rhythms appear more naturally irregular because they are
disregarding the formal regularity of the couplet-rhymes. And
this skillful, deliberate informalizing of a formal pattern, besides suggesting the reproduction of the actual rhythms of conversational speech, seems to echo as well the tone of the Duke's
confidences. He too is relaxing his usual proud formality on
this occasion, and we are aware both that this departure from

formality has some significance and that the formality is still there, though muted, in the background." [119]

Concluding his close examination of the verse form in *My Last Duchess,* Beatty wrote that "all the elements of poetic expression—foot, line, strophe, metre, or what not—are not [to be] considered as constituting an end in themselves; they are consistently [to be] regarded as the incarnation of the thought, emotion and action of the poem. We [see] how the various elements have an artistic significance only through their being the embodiment of the poet's thought; and how the form assumes Protean shapes in response to the demands of the informing spirit." [120]

It would seem a fine illustration of that "informal formality" that the Duke does not trouble to complete the two poetic 'sentences' he begins, as though in thorough contempt for the absurd position into which the Duchess' "heart . . . too soon made glad" has almost compelled him: "Even had you skill . . . to make . . . and say . . ."; and "and if she let/Herself be lessoned so, nor . . . set . . . and made. . . ." Then the dash preceding the summary clause ("—E'en then would be some stooping") and the 'sentences' begun remain only begun. His use of "you" (line 36) rather than the more formal and putatively appropriate 'one' would seem another instance of the subtle relaxation of his customary "rigidity" of manner; further, it has the force both of directly involving his listener (to include, perhaps, Browning's reader) and eliciting his support in recognizing the impossibility of the Duke's strange and unaccustomed position as one patently more frequently encountered in the base, even sordid, marriages of argument and equivocation, conciliation and compromise, among the commonalty. "Even" could "you make your will/Quite clear," could one aver the obvious, explain your rectitude, condescend to spell out what must to any other be eminently lucid, I could not be expected to do so. The degradation of the Duchess, her own baseness for Ferrara, ought to be manifest in his calling her "such an one"

—merely a woman, a 'wife,' easily duplicated several millionfold
in the world. How could *I*, he asks (and posits and sneers and
pleads and demands), be expected to tell her

> 'Just this
> Or that in you disgusts me; here you miss,
> Or there exceed the mark'?

Could *I* be expected to illuminate the obvious, to remember
or even to note as they occur specific instances of her identicality
of "rank," of her too-expansive gratitude? But even if I could—
(and most assuredly I could not)—compromise, abase myself by
elucidating such improprieties, she would—or *could*—not have
learned from my counsel.

> and if she let
> Herself be lessoned so, nor plainly set
> Her wits to yours, forsooth, and made excuse . . .

Apparently, the Duke had indeed attempted such counsel,
but she could not learn, "let/Herself be lessoned" by that counsel, "so"; quite to the contrary (and the "forsooth"—'indeed'—
is most derisive), she took exception to his advice, then his
instruction, then his admonition. Quite "plainly," she took
mild exception, she smiled innocently: 'But it *was* so nice of
him to give me the cherry bough,' 'But the sunset this evening
was so lovely,' 'But Bainardo *was* so delightful today.' There
was no truculence in her; the lady believed what she said; she
did not desire to argue with "her husband." But in offering
her "excuse," she "plainly set/Her wits to" the Duke's, "to
yours," to anyone's who would have been rational and so manifestly right. Apparently, she simply could not comprehend the
abstraction of the title, though she could see a sunset and love it.

He scorns his own 'hypothetical' argument by the impatient
dash (line 42); the rhetoric is so conjectural that he could not
'admit' to another argument that he might have offered. "Even
had you skill . . . and say . . ."; and "if she let/Herself be"

reasoned with, permitted herself to learn from her errors of
excess and not "set/Her wits to yours . . . and made excuse,"

> —E'en then would be some stooping; and I choose
> Never to stoop.

He cannot finish; he had then, and has now, absolutely no
patience for any "sort of trifling." The Duke's fragmentary
'sentences' here are emphasized poetically by especially marked
caesurae, which underscore his impatience with the lady.[121]
"E'en" to explain, clarify, admonish, attempt to instruct an in-
genuously refractory student, the Duke is saying, "would be
some," a little, "stooping"—for anyone; but for me, so to explain
would be a relegation of my grand name, of myself.

Burrows explained the Duke's problem: "What to do? Explain
his dissatisfaction to her? Talk the matter over with her? Teach
her the approved mode of conducting herself? A Duke of Ferrara
cannot lower himself to petty domestic counselling and correc-
tion. It would be derogatory to his dignity. It would involve
'some stooping'. . . ." [122] That "approved mode" is "that
solemn, aloof decorum which he believes essential to his exalted
rank and which demands the most rigid discrimination in the
receiving and conferring of favours and in deciding how a great
personage may properly feel, think, and behave." [123]

His eye holds the emissary's when he speaks these last six
words, and his brow clouds:

> . . . and I choose
> Never to stoop.

Let there be no mistake or misinterpretation, he seems to say;
I am the man who "commands" and expects, but I am not a
man who must demand, argue, explain, endeavor to persuade.
Can you comprehend this? I am not so much an independent
man as I am, like the Prince of Denmark, "subject to his
birth." [124] I have responsibilities and expectations over which
I do not exercise any personal control. I am the Duke of Ferrara.

It is my title that must "never" be allowed "to stoop"; and I privately owe all of my allegiance, my "will," my person itself, to that title. "I" *must* "choose/Never to stoop." [~~ 43

Neither Ophelia nor Lucrezia could comprehend the perhaps imperative subservience of the body natural of the man to the body politic of the prince. The next few lines account for an inevitability, perhaps, at least as much as a knowing cruelty, a necessity as much as a choice.

> Oh sir, she smiled, no doubt
> Whene'er I passed; but who passed without
> Much the same smile? This grew; I gave commands;
> Then all smiles stopped together. There she stands
> As if alive.

The extent to which the Duchess was a threat to the body politic of the Duke, however, would seem somewhat of a different matter from her threat to him personally. So far as she was unsuitable, incompetent—for whatever reasons—as the Duchess *per se,* she must be removed from that office. But that she undermined the heart of the man appears to be at the source of whatever profound insecurity Alfonso might have felt; two reasons but for one action. She did "like" him, since "her looks" alighted upon him, "her husband," as well as upon everything else. You must not misunderstand, he implies to the envoy; she did not ignore me, but rather she treated me with that horrible, enfeebling, intolerable "same"-ness; I was like all else to her. She could not comprehend my office—*what* I am. And she made me feel to be without any particular, unique, *personal* value; she totally dehumanized me. "No doubt" "she smiled" at me whenever we encountered each other; but in "much the same" manner did she smile at a page, a footman, a maid, a porter, a gardener, a secretary, an ostler—a sunset, a "white mule"! The "Oh sir" seems rather more a disguised plea for understanding, spoken with the Duke's customary elegant disdain and "patrician imperturbability" [125] than a mere interjection. She quite casually and effortlessly made him feel as though he were nothing, and, privately, he might have suspected that he was just that. "This" "same"-ness in her, "This" extemporaneous and unwitting scorn, "This" inability to learn, to mature, to comprehend who or what she was and I was— "This" "too soon made glad" "heart" only acquired new objects of appreciation; it became increasingly and pervasively manifest; it "grew."

It is well known that Browning himself, asked many years after he had written the poem, commented that "The commands were that she should be put to death . . . or he might have had her shut up in a convent." [126] W. C. DeVane noted, however, that "The poem far surpasses its source in subtlety and suggestiveness." [127] Corson, who had questioned Browning about the ambiguity, observed that the Duke "shut off her life currents, . . . and we must suppose that she then sank slowly and uncomplainingly away." He further noted that " 'I gave commands' certainly must not be understood to mean commands for her death. . . ." [128]

Friedland commended Corson's reluctance both to read the worst possible implications in the Duke's "commands" and to accept literally Browning's response: "Not even this Duke, addressing a Count's emissary come to arrange a match with his master's daughter or sister, would expect the listener to put the harshest construction on the words uttered. The Duke, we may believe, had found more subtle ways of accomplishing his aim with his Duchess; this is what his expression seems to imply. Too keen an art lover to shatter a precious *objet d'art,* he gives commands that constrain her to his sole possession. What if the Lady meanwhile dies of a broken heart? . . . Or, it may be, she took the veil, forever banished from life. To him her end is a matter of indifference." [129] Friedland offered an expansion of DeVane's comment in stating that "The creative artist is seldom able to recall the fleeting impressions that moved him to produce this or the other effect. Hence, while his comments on such effects, resulting from an attempt at recollection, are sure to be helpful, they are not at all times better than the instinctive perceptions of an acute critic like Corson." [130]

Most of the many commentators on the poem, however, agree with Browning that the Duke probably had the Duchess killed.[131]

Brooks *et al.* believed that the Duke either "had the Duchess killed or simply sent her away and let her die from humiliation and disgrace." [132] S. S. Curry stated, "It is doubtful whether she died of a broken heart or was deliberately murdered. His commands, of course, would not be given to her, but to his lackeys. Many think she was murdered. Browning leaves it artistically suggestive and uncertain." [133] And Burrows wrote that "The phrases harden into a lapidary abruptness and conciseness, and the base understatement [of "I gave commands"] plunges the reader into horrified conjecture: was she murdered? or incarcerated? or did she wither like a sensitive plant at a breath from a chilly wind? Guess on; the impressionable, delightful and delighting girl was crushed." [134]

Alexander commented that "In his own mind, [the Duke] represents her conduct as unbecoming her position, and determines to put an end to it. Coldly and relentlessly, the more cruelly that there is no outward violence, he proceeds to shape this tender creature to his own mould, but succeeds only in crushing hope, love, and life out of his young wife. She dies of a broken heart." [135]

In a rather wry, clumsy little comment entitled "Browning's Last Lost Duchess: A Purview," R. F. Fleissner offered the thesis that the Duke's "commands" and the permanent cessation of the Duchess' "smiles" do not necessarily constitute a sequitur— which thesis, probably, would render the Duke's conjoining the events as a remarkable bit of braggadocio before the envoy. "A completely plausible view," wrote Fleissner, "is that the Duke 'gave commands' to have her remedy herself whereupon she died; we know not what the interrelation might have been between the two events. We do know, however, that she was absent from him and that, during the course of this absence, she left this—as well as his—life." [136] The "commands" might mean "only that somehow an order or reprimand prohibited her from being offensive. No conclusive cause-and-effect relationship ought to be drawn other than that." [137] Fleissner, dismissing "an envenomed goblet" or her being "carted off to an alpine retreat," offered the possibility (and some ice water in the faces of the legions of Duke-haters) that the Duchess "was out of her wits, that she smiled a bit too much and thus had to be confined for the benefit of society [and, presumably, the Duke] in a madhouse. . . . That she passed away thereafter can be explained in terms of inhuman Renaissance asylum conditions [apparently including those to which a Duchess of Ferrara would be "confined"] or in terms of natural causes . . .; perhaps, indeed, she had a form of 'laughing sickness,' poetically a no less unpalatable assertion than that she was assassinated. So if the poor woman had gone insane, the Duke would have been officially forced [sic] to take legal action, to give commands to have her committed. As a last resort, we could always rely on the eventuality that she died of the bubonic plague." [138]

"The conclusion, then, is based on textual evidence and does not deny the possibility that the Duke was a possibly wicked, ruthless potentate. The trouble with such an inference is that to assert he was villainous is to probe more between the lines than the context of this dramatic monologue warrants. . . . We do not have to believe that the Duke killed his first wife or had her killed; to believe that he may, for some readers, even destroy the aesthetic value of the poem by making the central figure, the speaker, a disgusting personality. It is surely more wholesome to accept the text for what it is, and maintain that the Duke did take firm action, that his duchess simply was lost to him thereafter and died. We should no more try to read between the lines and ascertain exactly how she succumbed than we should expect to be able to look behind her portrait and determine whether or not she had a mole on the back of her neck!" [139]

But to some readers "reading between the lines" means to other readers reading the lines, trusting the poet, trusting the words. However, one does not know how to take Fleissner's pronouncements; they might be a scholar's rather cumbersome amusement, or one might hear a pained rumbling from beneath the floor of The Poets' Corner.

The nature of such "commands" as those given directly to end the lady's life might not seem consistent with the character of the Duke of Ferrara (if characters are to be considered consistent in or out of poetry): he might well be too elegant and subtle a man for such rather plebeian measures. So to be rid of her would indeed seem a somewhat overt admission of her victory over him in a warfare he had never sought, an admission of his succumbing to her thoughtless resistance, of his tacit recognition that apart from his title he was as much a personal cipher as that nameless, faceless "officious fool." Murdering her or even sending her to a convent, in fine, would be tantamount to "stooping" as far down as a man can go. But the Duke seems to desire that ambiguity: The emissary must report to the Count that such measures as the Duke *might* take with an unresponsive, nondiscriminating next Duchess *might* be extreme; and yet the Duke can hardly be attracting that next Duchess, together with her "munificent" dowry, were it known—or even seriously believed—that he had his "last" one murdered or banished in disgrace. He is guilty, however, of at least somewhat of a redundancy in "gave commands"; again he asserts his power, and he would have it clear that he would be quite capable of the most extreme measure of ducal displeasure.

An action that would seem commensurate with his overweening decorum and sophistication might be "commands" to seal her from "all and each," to curb those "looks" that "went everywhere": he had her locked in a small room, without sunlight or intercourse with servants, a dungeon suitable to a Duchess guilty of no 'crime' other than nebulous indiscretion. The measure of her delicacy and appreciative regard for all things, of her perhaps mindless and thoroughly sensuous happiness, is that "all smiles"—for her mule, her cherry blossoms, her Duke, her sunsets—"stopped together." She died of ennui and loneliness, almost "humiliation and disgrace." "Then" (line 46) has the force of 'therefore,' introducing a consequence the Duke might have considered was going to prove inevitable. The passage of time between the "commands" and her death, however, might not have been so short, although he very much wants to give the illusion of a quick and automatic result as a further instance of his displeasure and dramatic authority. And even now, "she stands/As if alive" behind her curtain-dungeon, and the Duke yet controls the drawpull.

IX

FOR a few seconds he turns his gaze at the portrait, the face, the eyes. He says,

> There she stands
> As if alive.

The pause between the first and last three words is subtle, elusive, indicated by no more than the end of the verse. His pause here between those calm words can almost freeze one's blood. Similarly, Lionel Stevenson wrote, "What actually happened to the Duchess is conveyed in the space between the words 'together' and 'There.' Any explicit statement about her doom would have been far less horrifying than this chilly hint." [140] Thomas Blackburn commented that "The innumerable possibilities . . . of those 'commands' by which the Duke stifled his wife's will to live are all the more sinister for being unspecified." [141] And Howard remarked that "Into these few words Browning has compressed a life's tragedy." [142]

Perhaps that silent envoy felt the grief and horror, but he (also) has not yet said a word. The Duke wishes to indicate that she is indeed dead but does not wish to speak so crude a word. He admits neither compunction nor contrition before his auditor, but his words and manner, authoritative and sure, indicate that her death had to be; he had done what was necessary—indeed, almost requisite.

He, then, refers to "her" as a painting once again, no longer as the woman about whom he had been speaking; once more "she" becomes a "piece," a "wonder" of portraiture; and the woman, who had been made to live again, retreats into the eternally frozen picture. The Duchess does not "stand"; the figure in the portrait does. The work is so much a "wonder, now" that it seems "As if" its subject were indeed "alive." The three dimensions become two once more, and the breath ceases, and the Duke pulls the cord that closes the curtains.[143] Once again the soft whir of the sliding mechanism, and once again he turns to the ambassador.

His tone is altered a bit now—slightly more peremptory, direct, official. "Will't please you rise?" he asks urbanely, just as a few minutes past he had asked—stated, ordered—"Will't please you sit . . . ? Directly, the ambassador stands, to await the Duke's pleasure. The latter takes a step before the curtains, in the direction of the stairs, saying,

> . . . We'll meet
> The company below, then.

"Then" again has the weight of 'therefore,' which would mean here that the Duke believes he has pellucidly made his point and that the envoy comprehends what is expected of him. The word might indicate also that the Duke has not said anything that he might now wish to retract—in word, emphasis, or implication. He has spoken well, and he knows it. The Duchess is once more in her usual state, hidden from the light, ostensibly gone as well from the Duke's consciousness.

"Below," with the "company," the two men will have no further opportunity for a 'discussion' of the immediate reason for the Count's emissary's visit to Ferrara, so the Duke takes these last moments of private 'conversation' to summarize his position. Those critics who have found the justification for these lines—even for the entire monologue—in the Duke's supposed avarice appear to have permitted personal revulsion to outweigh scrutiny. Assad argued well that the primary importance of these lines (48–53) is the literal one: the Duke intends in these words to declare that "(1) my pretense for dowry will be a just one, and (2) my chief desire is for the lady herself." [144]

The Duke is clear in indicating that all that remains to be decided is the size of the dowry, not whether the Count's "fair daughter" will indeed become the next Duchess or whether, after she is betrothed, she will have any doubt where most she owes obedience.

Only with "The Count your master" does Browning allow us to be informed that it is an envoy of another nobleman to whom the Duke has been speaking, and only with "dowry" and "fair daughter" do we learn the reason for the envoy's visit. ". . . The disclosure of [the speech's] purpose and of the identity of the Duke's listener is deliberately delayed until the very end. Once made, the disclosure is retroactive, charging what has gone before with deeper significance, and enabling us to lay the appropriate emphasis on 'last' in the title and the first line. . . ." [145]

> I repeat,
> The Count your master's known munificence
> Is ample warrant that no just pretence
> Of mine for dowry will be disallowed;
> Though his fair daughter's self, as I avowed
> At starting, is my object.

Let there be nothing in these arrangements, the Duke posits, so vulgar as equivocating about money. The envoy will remember those injunctions as well. The Duke recognizes the Count's generosity as "known" (a pleasantry that the Duke might hope is accurate); my stated offer, he avers, my "pretence," will be quite reasonable, "just"—as reasonable and "just" as I am (in *all* regards); but *senza dire*, it is the lady, not the dowry, that I desire. The noncommittal, nebulous "fair daughter" seems to indicate that the Duke has never seen the lady. (Similarly, he might trust as well that he will be proven reasonably accurate about her comeliness.) It is no "wife" that he wants, however, but a Duchess, and a considerable reward for offering her so splendid a match.

"He is desirous of a wife, not as a companion, but as a necessary ornament for his palace," wrote Cleanth Brooks *et al.*[146]
There are, however, major differences between a "wife" and
"companion," and a Duchess. The former might be an "ornament" of a man's private life; but the latter is an obligation of
his office, one that is quite independent of personal desires. Obviously, the more vital that office, the more urgent is that obligation. Absurdly often is the Duke condemned for not being a
simple Christian man, one with no responsibilities or duties
larger than himself. The "last" Duchess, the authors continued,
"was a natural, innocent woman whom the Duke could not bend
into the conventional form he thought his wife should have." [147]
Such a statement might seem more justifiable were the word
"conventional" changed to *necessary,* and "wife" to *Duchess.*
The "self" of the Count's "fair daughter" is similarly a Duch-
ess-designate and not a more "conventional" intended bride.
The Count would understand the distinction.

In the same regard, Langbaum's statement that the Duke
"is now about to contract a second marriage for the sake of
dowry" [148] is typical of the many commentators who ignore the
vital difference between the desired wife and the politically
requisite Duchess. Ferrara must have a Duchess; such is the
Duke's obligation, not prerogative (see Appendix A).

This display of eloquence certainly is not lost on the ambassador; the Duke's "skill/In speech" is no less than a prodigy:

> The Count your master's known munificence
> Is ample warrant that no just pretence
> Of mine for dowry will be disallowed;
> Though his fair daughter's self, as I avowed
> At starting, is my object.

"These lines are a masterpiece of diplomatic circumlocution,"
observed Perrine. "The nature of the demand is made amply
clear, yet it is gloved in a sentence softened by a double nega-
tive and by a skillfully tactful and euphemistic choice of diction:

not 'riches' but 'munificence'; not 'proves' but 'is ample warrant'; not 'my demand' but 'no just pretence of mine'; not 'refused' but 'disallowed.' The hard bargaining is thus enveloped
in an atmosphere of perfect courtesy and good breeding." [149]

Since the Duke speaks these words to "repeat" or summarize
what he had intimated before, when the two men were still in
private colloquy upstairs, he must have spoken then with even
more "diplomatic circumlocution," the subtlety of which is far
more an intellectual delight than an exasperating evasion.

The two men, walking slowly, the emissary his deferential
half-step behind the Duke, have reached the stairs leading down
to the great rooms where the "company" is gathered. That the
above five lines were spoken on the landing before they reached
the stairs seems perhaps the most convincing testimonial to the
Duke's fluency.

His Grace suddenly thrusts his arm behind the emissary's
shoulders, as though to prevent the latter's ambulatory homage
to his betters. He almost smiles as he elegantly protests this
small showing of the *noblesse oblige* he expects:

> Nay, we'll go
> Together down, sir.

But here is none of the spontaneity, gentlemanliness, and grace
in this line as there is in the words of Hamlet to Horatio and
Marcellus that it must inevitably echo: "Let us go in together"
(I.v.187). Rather, in this continuation of his counterfeit egali-
tarianism, the Duke is still the "commanding" lord whose prerogative it is occasionally to appear democratic, the more to
elicit that deference and obedience in others by calling attention
to his own perception of that deference and obedience.

George Monteiro termed the Duke's actions and words here
"a gesture of calculated munificence and quite possibly social
flattery";[150] and Perrine added that the effect probably succeeded.[151] Recall me to the Count, he seems to suggest to his
listener, as a liberal after all, as a demanding though complex,

eloquent, gracious, democratic, ultimately fair man, of *almost* infinite patience, and superlative taste.

As they move down the great staircase, the Duke, "with a casual off-handedness loaded with ulteriority," [152] nods the envoy's attention to a niche in the wall holding a small bronze: [153]

> Notice Neptune, though,
> Taming a sea-horse, thought a rarity,
> Which Claus of Innsbruck cast in bronze for me!

Patently, much is involved in the Duke's "suggestive carelessness" [154] in pointing out the sculpture. Monteiro viewed lines 48–53 as an intentional "act of excessive munificence" that thereby immediately calls attention to the bronze piece. "This gesture, as the Duke well knows, has the contextual effect of confirming in still another way his personal efficacy. For the Duke's drama of unconscious challenge and final domination is reenacted in the spacial conjunction of the two works." [155] Its being a "piece" of art causes the portrait of the Duchess further to recede into such designation. He wishes the envoy to take note that only as a "piece" is the portrait important to him, "now"; its subject, "now," would be only tangential to its being a "Frà Pandolf," just as this object is a "Claus of Innsbruck" primarily, a work depicting a particular subject only secondarily. [156]

The "though" seems to carry the weight of 'in spite of all I have said, remember only the substance as it concerns "The Count your master" and "his fair daughter" '; or, "though" has the import of 'also'—as though the Duke has pointed out one work of art, and 'here also is another, notable as the work of another celebrated artist, as further tangible evidence of my importance and superior taste.' The subject of the bronze certainly is also vital, since it is one that the Duke has ordered and so would not be any piece either inherited or arbitrarily acquired. Neptune, the supernal Earth-Shaker and Lord of the

Seas, by his power subdues a "sea-horse," in a way a quite feminine creature: what or who is there that is not subject to the Duke of Ferrara's "taming"?

Edward Berdoe found the piece an analogue to the Duke's situation in that "he had tamed and killed his last duchess." [157] And Friedland observed that "It has been suggested that the Duke points out this particular work of art in his gallery as a visual artistic symbol of how he curbed the last Duchess into submission, like Neptune taming a sea-horse." [158]

But the connection might be that Neptune is seen in an attitude of doing what the Duke cannot do, that the latter can only have order ed to be "cast" a symbol that might represent his desires in "taming," subjugating, vanquishing, bending to his will—or, in the form of a bronze group, his accomplishments in art impossible in his life.

Robert Graves, incidentally, found Neptune, or Poseidon, "of a surly, quarrelsome nature" [159] and H. J. Rose noted that he is "violent and ill-tempered." [160] He is sometimes credited with having created the horse, the bridle, and horse-racing, and having copulated with Demeter while both were in equine form. In Poseidon's stables in the Aegean, "he keeps white chariot horses with brazen hooves and golden manes." [161] "It is not at all certain that he was originally conceived as of human form; several legends and his standing title Hippios, 'He of the Horse(s),' are consistent with his having horse-shape." [162] Since the horse was sacred to Neptune (he fathered Pegasus, out of Medusa), the "taming" might have been done perhaps with less brutish violence than harshly expressed affection. Whether or not the Duke of Ferrara is aware of the possible ironies in the piece that he had "cast in bronze, for me!" would be an interesting issue. Monteiro observed that "the artist has happily cast the Duke as a mythological god. The Duke's pleasure in seeing himself in the guise of Neptune is evident, but what is more significant is that he has chosen to view himself in a show of force." [163]

As for the "tamed" figure's being a "sea-horse," Robert Spindler wrote: "If the speech here is about a 'sea-horse,' then it is meant to be one of Poseidon's horses which draw his chariot when he wants to travel over the billows of the sea." [164]

The piece was ordered probably prior to the advent of the "last" Duchess; otherwise, it would have depicted Neptune's "taming" a tetra. It is "thought a *rarity*" because of its unusual subject (see Appendix B) or especially detailed workmanship of fine tolerance, or both; and it is *"thought"* so since the Duke once more tries to "tame" the envoy by indicating to him that all men with a learned eye for the finest in art must recognize its excellence and singularity. This most diplomatic ambassador can only nod his assent.

The 'imaginary' "Claus of Innsbruck," of course, is an artist of the Tyrol of which the emissary represents the Count (see Appendix A). I, the Duke is also averring, possess some of the best of your region, so that my values, as well as my prospects and cosmopolitism, extend even there. "The Duke knows that he is addressing a gentleman from Innsbruck," wrote Friedland; "and as the two—Duke and emissary—are on their way out from the portrait-gallery, the Duke calls the other's attention to a piece of statuary: 'Observe this rarity, sir,—a work by your countryman, Claus of Innsbruck, the City in which you hold such high rank and the home, at present, of the Lady Barbara [see Appendix A] who, if all things go as I would have them, will share my nine-hundred-years-old name.' A fine bit of polished finesse, this! So characteristic of Browning, forever unerring in his psychologic instinct." [165] The patronizing, proprietary phrasing of "cast in bronze," as was mentioned above, is of the same order as his patronage of "Frà Pandolf": the intimation seems to be that the conception of "Neptune . . . taming a sea-horse" is quite exclusively the Duke's; 'only' the workmanship and the "cast[ing] in bronze" belong to the sculptor.

X

THREE people become alive and knowable in this poem, yet only one speaks, that stately, selfish, and subtle man whose monologue underscores his enforced loneliness and consciousness of who and what he is.[166] It would seem most typical that that man's monologue—so much of it as Browning has allowed us to overhear—ends with "for me!" No fewer than twenty times in this short poem does the Duke directly refer to himself.[167] The piece by "Claus of Innsbruck," my conception, he as much as states, was, like the portrait, done "for me!"

But such egotism might well provide just the surface manifestation of either a wealth of personal insecurity or an awareness that his personality—such as it might be—must always remain subordinate to the responsibilities of his office. He certainly does have the intelligence, and perhaps he has the rationality as well, to recognize that he is only a genetic accident, that the one born to assume the considerable duties of the Grand Duchy of Ferrara, the fortuitous inheritor of that "nine-hundred-years-old name," happens to be qualified by primogeniture alone and might actually be quite an ordinary man otherwise—vain, humorless, jealous, petty, insecure, morally mediocre, defensive, proud, selfish, joyless, limited, egoistical. The Duchess' portrait was painted and by the renowned and justly celebrated "Frà Pandolf," not only because of the Duke's superior artistic sensibilities but because portraits of the members of the House are a royal custom—indeed, such was, had been, and remains the fashion among the titled, as well as the merely solvent. The immediate subject of "Claus of Innsbruck's" sculpture might well have been of private import to the Duke, but so was Verrocchio's glorious equestrian monument to Bartolomeo Colleoni, or Botticelli's *Pallas Subduing the Centaur* to Lorenzo de' Medici. The Dukes of Ferrara have been, and continue in Browning's Duke to be, quite literally patrons of the arts. Perhaps the Duke thought the Duchy itself to have been compromised by a Duchess unsophisticated enough to prove an unworthy holder of the title; to him, the subject of a work of art is not wholly sufficient as its justification.

Possibly, however, for one to attempt an explanation of the Duke's actions in terms of his pervasive consciousness of his—and her—body politic might be inadequate regarding the poem Browning has written. Quite in addition to his subordination of all he was to his title, the Duke certainly does seem a rather brutal man. He caused the death of one woman (although he might have been, as least initially, inclining only to her reformation), and doubtless at least the extreme discomfort and enmity of many other persons. The subject of the Duke as ur-villain appears to predominate in most critical writings on the poem; we are told repeatedly that the evil of the Duke is notorious and luminous. The following examples may be taken as typical:

"The Duke . . . is one of the subtlest villains in English literature. It is easy enough to see that he has had his first wife killed. . . ." [168]

My Last Duchess is "a study in that vitality and unscrupulousness, that luxury and love of art, that cruelty and subtlety, [Browning] always associated with Italy and the Renaissance." [169]

". . . the theme is . . . the tyranny of a man over a woman —the tyrannical suppression of one nature by another; the jealous man who would control the smiles of his wife to himself alone—that imposition of tyranny on the soul which either makes it, as in 'The Little Duchess,' or breaks it, as in 'My Last

Duchess.' The one soul found emancipation through imagination and spiritual uprush to a region where human tyranny is powerless to pain; the other shrinks and dies, finding its release in death." [170]

The Duke is "a soulless *virtuoso*—a natural product of a proud, arrogant, and exclusive aristocracy . . . ," who has "weak pride," "fiendish jealousy," and "fossilized, contemptible meanness." The Duchess, quite on the contrary, is a woman of "sweetness and joyousness," "a generous soul-life," who is "pure, and fresh, and sparkling," "sweet and lovely." [171]

The Duke is "some accomplished devil" "displaying his wife's portrait as the wonder of his gallery, and unconcerned by disposing of her person." [172]

"Nothing can be subtler than the art whereby the Duke is made to reveal a cruel tragedy of which he was the relentless villain, to betray the blackness of his heart, and to suggest a companion-tragedy in his betrothal close at hand. Thus was introduced a new method, applied with such coolness as to suggest the idea of vivisection or morbid anatomy." [173]

". . . an Italian Duke of the Renascence lives in all his love of art, his pride, his cruelty so unhesitating and remorseless that it seems non-human rather than simply criminal." [174]

"The Duke . . . is a monster. He sacrifices a lovely and joyous creature on the altar of his vanity. He extinguishes a human life because it does not imitate and proclaim the perfection of his own. He murders joy and innocence, and murders selfishly and coldly. There is no heat in him, no passion, no real anger, only hurt vanity." [175]

". . . the icy refinement, the cold culture, the heartless pride and inhumanity of the duke are thrown into high relief by the glimpse he himself gives us of the sweet and simple-hearted girl whose too ready smile and gentle courtesy were her undoing." [176]

"*My Last Duchess* . . . shows us how detestable the Duke was, but the poor young Duchess must have been a charming girl, with her joyous, ever-ready smile and blush of thanks for the least courtesy, and sadly we think of her, crushed and drooping under her tyrannous husband." [177]

The Duke has also been called "this dealer in human souls," [178] a victim of "satanic pride" [179] and "psychopathic egoism," [180] "a predator," [181] "an arrogant, coldblooded, cruel tyrant," [182] and "a psychopathic murderer." [183]

The invective perhaps reaches its summit in the Duke's being regarded as "Inured to murder and ignorant of Christian virtues" and "clearly symbolic of the pride, materialism, and viciousness of Christian evil, so filled with *hubris* that he is wantonly and sadistically destructive, and, ironically, blind to his probable damnation." [184] And another critic saw the evil of the Duke as so bountiful that it includes an immediate threat even to the life of the Count's envoy (who, apparently, also "smiles" too much): "Why did [the Duke] say all this to such a person? To overawe him, to show him what kind of man he had to deal with, and the necessity of accepting the Duke's terms lest 'commands' might also be given regarding him, and his 'smiles' stop, like those of the lovely Duchess." [185]

Perhaps the critics likewise protest too much. "Even the married male reader," commented Burrows, "will surely find the Duchess' punishment disproportionate to her 'crime.' The Duke's narrow and uncompromising code is bound to excite revulsion in Browning's audience; the ruthlessness with which he crushes her excites horror; the calm, complacent assurance with which he recounts her story intensifies both horror and revulsion." [186]

That part of Browning's "audience" certainly was represented by William Lyon Phelps, an earlier generation's middlebrow's highbrow, whose detestation of the Duke now might seem only amusingly vituperative if it did not have such broad currency among readers over the years:

"The Duke tells the envoy that his late Duchess was flirtatious, plebeian in her enthusiasm, not sufficiently careful to please her husband; but the evident truth is that he had a Satanic pride, that he was yellow with jealousy, that he was methodically cruel. . . .

"What difference does it make whether he poisoned her, or whether he simply broke her heart by the daily chill of silent contempt? For her, at all events, death must have been a release. She would have been happier with a drunken husband, with a brute who kicked her, rather than with this supercilious cold-hearted patrician. Toward the end of the poem, in his remarks about the dowry, we see that the Duke is as avaricious as he is cruel; though he says with a disagreeable smile, that the woman herself is his real object. . . . ."

Finally, in one of the neater tricks of the early part of the century, "Only once or twice do we see the teeth of this monster flash, revealing his horrible heart." [187]

The last two mentioned writers did not strengthen their cases with their mellifluous observations of the contrasting Duchess—whose desirability seems to diminish with each saccharine word or phrase:

". . . with her pretty thanks and her prettier blushes, the Duchess is unmistakably a supremely delightful and delighting girl, loved and admired by all except her husband. She is, as the Duke would scorn to be, warm, friendly, lively, human, natural." [188]

"I suppose she was really a frank, charming girl, who came from a happy home [quite likely the Palazzo Vecchio, by the way], a bright and eager bride; she was one of those lovely women whose kindness and responsiveness are as natural as the sunlight. She loved to watch the sunset from the terrace; she loved to pet the white mule; she was delighted when some one brought her a gift of cherries. Then she was puzzled, bewildered, when she found that all her expressions of delight in life received a cold, disapproving glance of scorn from her husband; her lively talk at dinner, her return from a ride, flushed and eager, met invariably this icy stare of hatred." [189]

But perhaps it is only a sad, grievous, bitterly pained man who heaps protest upon protest in his "choice" "never" to demean his nobility. He is doubtless perceptive, and might well be aware that his pomposity and "choos[ing]/Never to stoop" would appear largely all he has. He remains suspicious, frigid, implacable, dominant, absolute—all apparently unattractive qualities to others.

But he is also immensely subtle and devastatingly eloquent. He speaks but little and intimates a volume on the complexities of humanity.

Moreover, most of the commentators who find the Duke so evil, tyrannous, and "soulless" do not seem to consider the form of the poem as a vital adjunct to the major persona's words: he is speaking to another man, quite consciously presenting the rationale of his own behavior and attitudes; he must appear at least a bit more implacable in his regard of his "last Duchess" if he is to be tolerably pleased in the necessary ducal boredom with the commonplace in his next Duchess; and he often enough speaks in tones that might be almost grievous about what he considered he *had* to do to the late Duchess. After all, nowhere does he exhibit any hatred, or even dislike, of the lady. Were he capable of less formality and were he speaking to a confidant, he might well seem somewhat more sympathetic, and the genuine tragedy of the situation be more lucid. One must consider all the implications in the observation, so full of meaning and so compact, that "The Duke's talk is carefully calculated to impress the envoy." [190] As was stated at the outset, the poem is not a narrative, *or* a monologue, in limbo.

At its original publication in *Dramatic Lyrics* in 1842, Browning entitled this poem "Italy," as he entitled *Count Gismond* "France." [191] He intended, rather, Renaissance Italy—or better, The Renaissance.[192] The poem, noted S. A. Brooke, "is plainly placed in the midst of the period of the Renaissance by the word *Ferrara,* which is added to the title. But it is rather a picture of two temperaments which may exist in any cultivated society, and at any modern time. But there are numbers of such men as the Duke and such women as the Duchess in our midst. Both are, however, drawn with mastery. Browning has rarely done his work with more insight, with greater keenness of portraiture, with happier brevity and selection." [193]

H. C. Duffin stated the case excellently when he wrote that in the poem is "not only the character of an epoch, and a complex situation within that epoch, delineated absolutely, and with ease and economy, but a sheer triumph of form. . . ." [194] He compared the poem to a "Chopin prelude or a water-colour by Turner." [195] But perhaps at this point in the present study it might be more germane for one to think of the work as being less pastel and much more akin to a piece by Bach (perhaps the *Italian Concerto*); or one of Lorenzo Lotto's "psychological portraits" (for example, the *Gentleman* in the Venice Accademia, or *Andrea Odoni* in the Royal Collection at Windsor), or perhaps a Holbein (*Bonifacius Amerbach* in the Basel Kunstmuseum, or one of his many studies of Henry VIII—in Warwick Castle, the Rome Galleria Nazionale, the London National Portrait Gallery, the Thyssen Collection in Lugano, etc.), or a Pontormo (*A Halberdier* in the Stillman Collection in New York, or *Cosimo de' Medici* in the Uffizi, or the incredible *Monsignor della Casa* in the National Gallery of Art in Washington).

The Renaissance was a time in which such men as the Duke of Ferrara—magisterial, fierce, elegant men—employed as subservient craftsmen and almost court entertainers and occasional aesthetic adjuncts to their rule and primary occupation of statecraft the painters, sculptors, poets, musicians, and architects whose work has reasonably given places in an historical accounting of the race to those men who patronized them. Unaware of the tenuousness of even his own House and dukedom and title, unaware of the permanence of art and the "awful brevity" of the individual life, the Duke, with his silent listener, leaves in that curious ellipsis, such as Browning wrote as the ends of many of his greatest dramatic monologues. Those endings perhaps only seem to lead into further words—of the speakers if not of the poems. But what might be more important, those endings mark the climax of the poems and leave the speakers in the attitude of their essences, in the summary of their souls, upon which Browning has allowed them to expatiate throughout the entire monologue. Lippo looks toward the first light of dawn over "this fair town's face" and says "Zooks!" and walks away, soberly, proudly, but a little sadly; Andrea tells his "Love" to "go" and then sits, "Quietly, quietly, the evening through," brooding on the waste, the folly, the irrevocable tragedy of his life; the Bishop of St. Praxed's closes his eyes peacefully, his glorious tomb forgotten, but in final triumph over his long-dead rival, almost inaudibly hisses "so fair she was!", and quietly dies.

The Duke of Ferrara moves down the grand staircase in that awesome palazzo, his words fading as he perhaps indicates another of his treasures or staidly greets one of the humble, expectant "company below." The small drama—and it is barely five minutes long—is over, and the actors disappear. From behind her darkening curtains "the faint/Half-flush that dies along her throat" and that gentle "spot of joy" in "the Duchess' cheek" will remain undiminished when her imperious Duke, like the lady herself, is dust and ashes.

Alfonso II d'Este

Friedland's study of the relationship between incidents inherent and intimated in *My Last Duchess* and the circumstances of the life of Alfonso d'Este, Duke Alfonso II of Ferrara (1533–1597; ruled 1559–1597), written in rebuttal of J. D. Rea's thesis that the model for Browning's Duke was Vespasiano Gonzaga, Duke of Sabbionetta (1531–1591), has subsequently come to be almost universally accepted as definitive.[196] In a nutshell, Friedland's researches discovered that in 1558 Alfonso married Lucrezia de' Medici (b. 1544), daughter of Grand Duke Cosimo I of Florence and Eleanora di Toledo (whose older daughter Maria, 1540–1557, was originally betrothed to Alfonso but who died, probably of spotted fever, before the wedding could take place). Lucrezia was then fourteen, Alfonso twenty-five. [Lucrezia had as a child possibly been promised in marriage to a "nephew" of Pope Julius III, Fabriano del Monte, but he died before the Medicis were able to make this particular political union.][197] Friedland quoted the historian Gaetano Pieraccini as noting that Lucrezia was "tall, thin, of modest mental endowment and not very much education, serious, very devout, but taciturn and by no means expansive; for this reason, her father called her by the nickname of '*Sodona!*' (obstinate), and because of her nature he often repeated: '*Costei è proprio de' nostri!*' (This one takes after us!)."[198]

Almost immediately following the marriage ceremony, Alfonso went to France (where he had spent much of his youth), without his wife (who remained in Florence), and stayed there for about two years, returning a year after the death of his father, Ercole II, to Lucrezia and his duties as the new Duke of Ferrara; he took the title of Alfonso II. Lucrezia died in 1561, aged seventeen, of uncertain causes; but it is to be noted that she had been ill a long while, "suffered from chronic lung-trouble," "Cosimo sent his court-physician to Ferrara to attend her," and "it is difficult to believe that Alfonso was so rash as to poison the young daughter of the powerful Cosimo, his near neighbor and a man not to be trifled with." [199] Friedland wrote that "It appears quite possible that her brief and sorrowful career and her pathetic end suggested to Browning the Duchess of his poem. In his monologue, no breath of scandal attaches to the pure and almost virginal lady, no fleshly love for some other man to arouse the jealousy of her husband. Youthfulness, un-spoiled simplicity are the essence of her character." [200] Fried-land quoted another historian, Chledowski, on Alfonso: "He was immoderately arrogant and conceited, and prided himself beyond measure upon his bravery, intelligence, and ancient descent. With all that he was vengeful and ever ready to pursue a feud." [201]

Alfonso married for the second time in 1565. His new Duch-ess was Barbara, sixth daughter of Ferdinand I, Count of Tyrol (the capital of which was at Innsbruck), who died in 1564 and was succeeded by his son Maximilian II. The negotiations for this union were interrupted by Ferdinand's death, but Barbara's brother Maximilian gave his assent, and Barbara and Alfonso were finally married. The accredited emissary of Maximilian was one Nikolaus Madruz [or, Cristoforo Madruzzo], who came from Innsbruck to arrange most of the negotiations of this rather intricate political union.

Barbara died in 1572. Alfonso married for the third time in 1577, his consort then being Margherita Gonzaga (the daughter of Barbara's sister Eleanora, Duchess of Mantua, and hence Alfonso's niece). Margherita outlived her Duke by twenty years, dying in 1618. Alfonso II, the "last of the Dukes of Ferrara" [202] died childless (see below).

In answer to Friedland's question of "How, then, did the poet receive the suggestion for the setting of his monologue?",[203] Stevens eschewed Friedland's suggestion of Bartolommeo Faccini's fresco portraits at the Castello Estense (see Appendix B) in favor of the thesis that Browning had found extremely suggestive material in an anecdote in Nathaniel Wanley's *Wonders of the Little World* (1806 edition), "with which Browning was certainly familiar." [204] The story recounts that the Duke of Ferrara enlisted the aid of a painter, Cesare Arethusi (?–1612) to sketch and then paint a portrait of a lady of the city without her knowledge, and " 'to preserve it from every eye except his [i.e., the Duke's] own.' " [205] Arethusi did the work but " 'thought it would be injurious to his fame to conceal from the world a performance which he accounted perfect. Through an excess of pride and vanity, he privately showed [the portrait] to several of his friends, who could not avoid commending the work. . . .' " [206] The " 'secret . . . circulated expeditiously,' " and the lady found out about the clandestine portrait, and the " 'enraged' " Duke almost had Arethusi killed but " 'only banished him for ever from his dominions.' " [207]

"Although the dissimilarities between the anecdote and the poem are many and obvious," noted Stevens, "there is a suggestive similarity that clutches at one's attention. If the Wanley story is indeed a source for the poem, it suggests that Browning was perhaps but remotely conscious of its influence and hence demonstrates the great degree of the freedom of the poet's imagination as it grasped at familiar fragments here and there from history [Friedland's sources] and anecdote and fused them into a new synthesis that was neither history nor anecdote—but poetry." [208]

Stevens cited as similarities between *My Last Duchess* and the Wanley anecdote the duke's being of Ferrara, Arethusi's possible connection with Alfonso II, the idea of banishment (although of the artist) "for showing off the portrait of which the duke has said, in effect, 'none puts by/The curtain . . . but I.' " [209] Stevens summarized his proposition by stating that "The duke of Wanley's tale, then, is the same as the one that Friedland has identified as Browning's." [210]

"Browning's wish in the poem, however, is to capture the essence both of a culture and of a certain kind of individual mind in a single representative character. He therefore transforms the story, either consciously or subconsciously, to suit his own needs. Whether or not he actually did realize, as well he might have, who the duke in Wanley's story was, he at least has access in it to the germ of an idea for a poem which would reveal the glittering decadence of a renaissance aristocrat such as he knew Alfonso to be. He knew from history Alfonso's scandalous behavior toward his first wife, Lucrezia, around whose death history's rumors have embroidered a mystery. [Friedland mentioned, and various Medici and Este family histories reveal, no such "scandalous behavior" and no evidence for any such "rumors"; the lady apparently died a natural, if premature, death.] The Wanley story gave him access to the idea of a duke of Ferrara's interest in a secret portrait of a lovely lady; Browning related this exquisite taste for the beautiful to Alfonso's known misbehavior [?] and provides us with a uniquely interesting psychological study." [211]

Pilkington's *A General Dictionary of Painters* (1824) lists a Cesare Arethusi, a Sixteenth Century Bolognese or Modenese portrait painter whose better work somewhat resembles that of Correggio and whose "principal patron was the Duke of Ferrara." [212] Pilkington here mentioned, and in the 1770 *The Gentleman's and Connoisseur's Dictionary of Painters* (pp. 20–21) wrote almost verbatim, the same story of the secret painting that Wanley reported.[213]

A few points mentioned by Friedland want some qualification here. Because of the arresting connections between Alfonso II and Browning's Duke, Friedland's researches led him to believe that "the Duke's pride in his 'nine-hundred-years-old name' is an inherited emotion, and to that extent pardonable. . . ." [214] He cited the year 1309 as the earliest one to which an Este (through the Gonzaga) can be traced. However, Alberto Azzo II (otherwise known as Marchese Alberto Azzo, or Marchese d'Italia, Conte della Lunigiana) was the first to have adopted the name Este (after the town some thirty miles north of Ferrara); he is also called Alberto Este, his dates being ca. 996–1097 [sic].[215] Alberto Este's line can be traced back to Bonifazio I, Conte di Lucca, Duca della Toscana, who flourished at about the end of the Eighth and beginning of the Ninth centuries. Ludovico Muratori cited a Papal bull for the founding of a monastery in the year 812, to which document one finds the signature of "Bonifatius Dux," reasonably establishing his birth at a considerable number of years prior to that date. Muratori wrote: *"In quest'anno, secondo il Fiorentini, Adalardo abbate di Corbeia, e messo di Carlo imperadore, quel medesimo che principalmente governava allora l'Italia nella minorità del re Bernardo, trovandosi nella città di Lucca, tenne un placito per la causa di un clerico delinquente, 'quem ipse Adalardus commendavit Bonifatio Illustrissimo Comiti nostro.' Sicchè conte di Lucca era allora questo Bonifazio, del quale, come di personaggio molto importante, io debbo far memoria. E ch'egli ancora fosse duca della Toscana, l'ho provato altrove con un placito del medesimo Adalardo abbate, tenuto in Pistoia nell'anno 812, al quale intervenne 'Bonifatius Dux.' "* ["In this year, according to Fiorentini, Adalardo, Abbé of Corbeia and envoy of Emperor Carlo (who was the principal ruler of Italy during the lesser reign of King Bernardo), was dispatched to Lucca to conduct a council in the case of a delinquent cleric, 'whom Adalardus himself entrusted to Our Most Illustrious Friend Bonifatius.' So that at that time the Count of Lucca was Bonifazio, of whom I must make mention as an extremely important individual; and that he was still Duke of Tuscany I have proved elsewhere by citation of a decree of the same Abbé Adalardo conducted in Pistoia in the year 812, at which there attended 'Bonifatius Dux.' "] [216]

In addition, there is reliable evidence that Bonifazio I's son, Bonifazio II, was born in the year 811.[217]

If Browning had such a history in mind, the "nine-hundred-years" antiquity of which the Duke boasts might not be too much of an exaggeration, or "an inherited emotion."

As Friedland noted, Alfonso died childless. The primary obligation of his body politic—to ensure the continuation of the dynasty by providing an unmistakable heir—was, then, a most ironical failure. But Friedland did not mention that Alfonso probably knew that he would leave no direct descendants. The popular belief in Ferrara, and in those times, was that because of a genital wound suffered in a tournament in France long before, he remained impotent throughout his adult life; Pieraccini's statement might be taken as typical of the belief: *"La Lucrezia fu una sposa sterile anche le altre due donne, cui legalmente si unì dopo la morte della Lucrezia. Anzi si desse allora che Alfonso fosse fatto impotente a generare da una ferita riportata ai genitale in un torneo in Francia."* ["Lucrezia remained a sterile spouse, as did the other two women to whom he was legally joined after Lucrezia's death. It was said even then that Alfonso was incapable of procreation because of a wound to his genitals suffered in a tournament in France."] [218]

However, Luciano Chiappini, who had access to a number of vital contemporary documents and who has written probably the definitive history of the Este family, dismissed the possibility of a tournament wound to Alfonso. Chiappini cited a document written by Girolamo Brasavola, special court physician to Alfonso, a report now in the Biblioteca Estense in Modena. This document *"tratta di una serie di annotazioni attorno alla figura clinica ed alle malattie o ai disturbi del duca di Ferrara. A chiare lettere vi è asserita la sterilità di Alfonso II, non acquisita ma congenita e tale da lasciare intatte tutte le normali manifestazioni fisiologiche. . . ."* [The document "discloses a series of notes concerning the clinical condition and ailments or disorders of the Duke of Ferrara. It asserts beyond a doubt the sterility of Alfonso II, not acquired but congenital, and as such left all normal physiological manifestations intact. . . ."] [219] Apparently, even when he was a fairly young man and shortly after his assumption, Alfonso recognized his inability to father an heir.

However, it was not directly owing to his having died without issue that Alfonso was responsible for the territorial loss of the Duchy of Ferrara to the Pope, nor was Alfonso the last of the House of Este. In 1567 a Bull of Pope Pius V, tacitly recognizing that Alfonso would leave no lineal heir, designated the return of the Ferrara Duchy to Papal fiefdom; the Bull thereby refused to grant Alfonso permission to name a successor. Alfonso, however, nominated his cousin Cesare (called Trotti), the son of Ercole II's brother don Alfonso, and petitioned a succession of Popes (Gregorius XIII, Sixtus V, Urbanus VII, and Gregorius XIV) for approval. His designation of Cesare was about to be accepted by Pope Gregorius XIV, but the Pope died before his Bull was promulgated, and Pope Clement VIII refused to recognize the legitimacy of Cesare. A clandestine treaty that Clement had made with Cesare's sister Lucrezia della Rovere, Duchess of Urbino, apparently was a major consideration in his refusal to grant the Este line a continuance on the throne of Ferrara.[220]

Furthermore, the Italian Estes did not die out until Ercole III Rinaldo in 1803; and the male line of the Austrian branch of the family lasted until 1875.[221]

Perhaps a few words more might be said about the intelligence of Lucrezia de' Medici, since Friedland did not seem to offer enough of what had been stated by Pieraccini—who, although quite politic and chivalric, established her rather marked limitations. She, alas, had much difficulty in writing even the alphabet, benefited nothing from the finest tutors, was absurdly superstitious, and was (perhaps for these reasons) infrequently allowed to leave her home even for short walks. She was far more sullen than joyous.[222]

Alfonso II was a diametric contrast. He was a highly intelligent and learned man. Although exuberant and given to elaborate carnivals, sporting events, masked balls, feasting, and such when young, he became more somber and incommunicative as he grew older. Difficulties with his anti-Papist mother, the early death of his second Duchess Barbara (whom Alfonso apparently loved a good deal), an unsuccessful campaign to claim the throne of Poland, increasing problems brought about by his inability to leave a primogenital heir, the refusal of successive Popes to recognize his designation of Cesare d'Este—all of these misfortunes left an embittered, grievous man. For the last several years of his life, he lived in virtual solitude, uncaring about the fortunes of the state he knew would be in his family no longer after he died.[223]

*   *   *

A far less relevant, and without too much doubt far less accurate, consideration is the one that purports that the portrait of the poem had been based upon one of Browning's grandmother: "It may perhaps throw a little personal interest around this portrait, when we observe that the picture Browning had in view, even to the hectic flush [by which one supposes the critic intends "that spot of joy"], is the likeness of his *grandmother* [italics his] hanging in the poet's study." [224]

Painting and Sculpture

Friedland did accurately mention that "In 1559, shortly after his assumption to the dukedom, Alfonso ordered his court painter, Bartolommeo Faccini to cover [a few of] the walls of the castle with lifesize portraits of the princely ancestors. This task Faccini accomplished with the help of his brother Girolamo and the painter Sebastiano Filippi, called Bastianini. . . . The painter worked in monochrome tints, *en grisaille*, or camayeu, as artists call it; there were many panels, each consisting of two figures, and of these not more than three groups were recognizable in Browning's time. Unfortunately, there is no statement to the effect that Faccini painted an al fresco panel of Alfonso II and Lucrezia." [225] Far more speculatively, Friedland added that "Nevertheless, we may think that Browning knew of these murals in the famous Castello of Ferrara and that Faccini's frescos came readily to his mind when he was meditating on Alfonso and the sad fate of the young Lucrezia." [226] However, Bartolommeo Faccini was not a notable painter either in his own time or subsequently, and the frescos of the Estes that he painted were not well known even to Renaissance scholars. But what would be far more important, Angelo Solerti, after viewing the walls of the Castello in the 1890's, wrote of the Faccini frescos as "vaguely distinguishable" [*"Sui muri della corte maggiore del Castello si distinguono vagamente dei resti di pitture d'un tono giallastro."*], only three groups of figures having been restored in Solerti's time, some decades after Brown-

Ferrara - Facciata del Castello - Monumento a Girolamo Savonarola

Castello Estense, Ferrara

ing could possibly have known of them.[227] The Salone dei Giochi (Large Game Room) of the Castello contains (as it did, of course, in Browning's time) the only extensive remains of the work of Sebastiano Filippi and *his* brother Camillo. Furthermore, Pilkington does not mention either Bartolommeo or Girolamo Faccini; the closest he comes is Pietro Facini, who lived ca. 1560–1602 and was a middling Bolognese student of Annibale Carracci.[228] It would then be reasonable for one to assume that Browning knew nothing of the few surviving Bartolommeo Faccini fragments; in other words, his reading or other knowledge did not commit him to an al fresco representation for his Duchess.

At any rate, fresco painting does not permit the obvious *sfumato* and *chiaroscuro* that "the faint/Half-flush that dies along her throat" and "that spot of joy" demand; such subtle shading would be quite the exception in a mural work; the fragments of the remaining Faccini portraits have no discernible shading. Almost all the known Este portraits are either on canvas or (usually for the early or middle *quattrocento* ones) wood; all are quite movable, and today are in many of the great museums of Italy and throughout Western Europe.

It is also important to one's understanding of the situation that the Duke has had this particular portrait of his Duchess moved to a place where either he or a "stranger" can readily "sit and look at" it. No necessary haste for completion, as would be required in much fresco work, is indicated for "Frà Pandolf's hands," which would have had both to plaster and paint; moreover, some fresco painting can be done a small section, no more than a few inches square, at a time.

Out of the immediate context of the poem, mural oil painting, which does contain some *sfumato* and *chiaroscuro* effects, was extremely rare and intricate—and time-consuming—and practiced by only a very few *cinquecento* artists—Sebastiano del Piombo (who is often credited with having conceived of the technique), Giorgio Vasari, Giulio Romano.[229] Generally, frescos in Renaissance Italy (as Browning and his Duke of Ferrara, artists' patron on a grand scale, must have known) depict large, crowded scenes—e.g., the Journey of the Magi, tournaments, battles, processions, the Last Supper—or separate panels arranged to portray sequential scenes—e.g., the Stations of the Cross, the lives of the saints. In addition, though there are a number of extant frescoed rooms and hallways in the Castello Estense, no mural oil portraits either remain or are known to have been painted there.[230]

The Duchess' portrait, *hanging* "on the wall" that the Duke had chosen, was, then, quite probably an oil painting. Although Browning had not seen them up to the time of his composition of *My Last Duchess,* he might have seen reproductions of two or three portraits that might be mentioned here. At the least, readers of the poem might find them of some interest. In apparently the late 1550's Agnolo Bronzino (1503–1572) painted a portrait of Lucrezia de' Medici, now in the Uffizi in Florence; copies of this work, probably by his student Alessandro Allori (1535–1607; he took the name Il Bronzino after the death of his great master), are in Poggio Imperiale, just outside Florence, and in the Kunsthistorisches Museum in Vienna. The Kunsthistorisches Museum copy (Inv. No. 2583) seems to be the only one of these works available for scrutiny; it is a large, three-quarter standing portrait labeled *Lucrezia oder Maria de Medici.* The figure is elaborately dressed, with jewel-encrusted strands of pearls about her waist, bodice, and hair; a plain strand of pearls encircles her throat. Her right hand holds a small book and her left what seems to be a pair of gloves, both items rather awkwardly. The background is elegantly plain. She appears to be somewhat shy and innocent, and young— perhaps fifteen or sixteen; she does not seem quite comfortable in the elaborate clothing. The face and neck are exquisitely shaded, and the dark eyes lustrous, the "spot of joy" most apparent, though the expression has distinct undertones of sadness. The work measures 114.5 by 89.5 centimeters and is

Portrait of Lucrezia de' Medici at 15 or 16 years. Attributed to Allori.
c. 1560.
(Courtesy Kunsthistorisches Museum, Vienna)

painted on poplar. The portrait (together with a miniature of it, also in the Kunsthistorisches Museum, painted by an unknown Austrian artist) has been in Vienna since at least the Seventeenth Century, so doubtless Browning did not see it before 1842, if at all. But perhaps it might be more than fancy for one to envision the "last Duchess" as Bronzino or Allori has done in this extraordinary painting.

Another work, now in the Pitti in Florence (Inv. No. 277) and possibly by Bronzino, though again more likely by Allori, depicts Lucrezia in "Three-quarters length. She is seen standing by a marble table wearing a rich dress sewn with pearls. Her left hand rests on a globe lying on the table; with her right hand she plays with a pendant at her throat. [As in the Vienna work] Her hair is parted and drawn back. She looks at the spectator." [231] This work, on a tin, pewter, or zinc base, is small, about 24 by 18 centimeters. Arthur McComb dated the work between 1558 and 1561, whereas Hanns Schulze mentioned 1560. A miniature of Lucrezia, in three-quarter profile and with other slight variations, is in the Uffizi. C. H. Smyth noted that Bronzino painted at Pesaro for Ercole II, Alfonso's father.[232]

Mention should also be made of a few portraits of the Duke himself. Most notable is one, by an unknown artist, in the Palazzo Doria in Rome; he is seen here as an old man in dark, austere raiment, far more tragic than brutal in aspect.[233] There is—or was—also a portrait of Alfonso probably erroneously attributed to Dosso Dossi, court painter to the Estensi in the early Sixteenth Century; in this portrait Alfonso is depicted as a young man nobly posed in armor, his left hand resting on the sheath of his sword, his right on a morion or jousting helmet on the table beside him.[234] Dosso (or Palmezzano) might also have painted Alfonso at the age of seven; that portrait is now in the Lord Wimbourne Collection at Ashby St. Ledgers, England.[235]

A number of contemporary bronze medals of Lucrezia and Alfonso exist. Perhaps most notable is the collection of the De-

*Alfonso II d'Este, Duke of Ferrara. Palazzo Doria, Rome.
(Courtesy Alinari, Florence)*

Medals by Pastorino da Siena, c. 1560. Lucrezia de' Medici,
Alfonso de' Medici
(Courtesy Department of Coins and Melals, British Museum,
London)

partment of Coins and Medals in the British Museum. Of those works, Lucrezia is seen on Nos. 473, 474, 475, and 476—No. 473 probably being the finest; that bronze medal is presently on exhibit in Room XXII, King Edward Gallery. Nos. 454, 455, and 456 depict Alfonso. All of those works are by Pastorino da Siena (or, Pastorino Pastorini; 1508–1592).[236] (Pastorino also worked medals of Alfonso's second Duchess, Barbara d'Autriche d'Este; they are Nos. 458, 459, and 460.) Two other medals (Nos. 800 and 801) of Alfonso are superb works by an unknown sculptor. Francesco Salviati (1510–1563) as well sculpted a bronze medal of Lucrezia as part of a series of medals that was to depict all of the vast Medici line; that piece is now in the Heberden Coin Room at the Ashmolean Museum, Oxford. The Ashmolean and the National Gallery of Art, Washington, also have casts of a remarkable work, Domenico Poggini's (1520–1590) medal of both Alfonso (obverse) and Lucrezia (reverse).[237]

*   *   *

The subject of Neptune's domination of aquatic creatures, scarcely unknown in Renaissance sculpture, would seem hardly "a rarity." The Frick Collection in New York has a *Neptune on a Sea Monster,* variously attributed to The Master of the Dragon and Severo da Ravenna, a Paduan who flourished about the beginning of the Sixteenth Century. The National Gallery of Art in Washington owns an almost identical piece, attributed to Severo da Ravenna.[238] Nearly identical pieces, or perhaps castings from the same mold, and also attributed to Severo, are currently in the Kunsthistorisches Museum in Vienna, the Museo Nazionale in Florence, and the Blumka Collection in New York.[239] All of those bronzes are about eighteen inches from the base to the top of Neptune's trident.

The Victoria and Albert Museum, London, has a remarkable piece, a bronze of (and there could be no more pertinent description) "Neptune . . ./Taming a sea-horse," attributed to Alessandro Vittoria (1525–1608), a renowned Venetian sculptor.

Neptune by Alessandro Vittoria. c. 1575.
(Courtesy Victoria and Albert Museum, London)

The work, which has lost its trident, stands about nineteen inches high. It appears to have been acquired by the Victoria and Albert in 1910, but so far its location before that date cannot be traced; whether that piece was known to Browning must remain, at least temporarily, conjectural. In the work, Neptune appears quite stern and determined, and the "sea-horse" gentle, delicate, feminine, submissive.[240]

Apparently, Isabella d'Este (grandaunt of Alfonso II) owned a similar work, *"Un Neptuno sopra un monstro col tridente,"* which might have remained in Ferrara, or in Mantua, at least until Alfonso's time.[241]

Friedland noted that "Browning visited Innsbruck and the Tyrol four years before the first appearance in print of *My Last Duchess,* when he was on his way home from his summer excursion to Italy in 1838. One is unable to conclude from this that he saw a work of sculpture there which he recalls in the poem. And yet, many years later, he describes in *The Ring and the Book* a work of art he saw in Russia, at the Hermitage, during a trip [1834] preceding that to Italy.[242]

In Stevens' discovery of a possible source of the Duchess' painting (see Appendix A), Wanley's *Wonders of the Little World,* he found, but one page later, the following:

> Scopas deserveth praise for his worthy workmanship, in which most account is made of those images in the chapel of Cn. Domitius in the cirque of Flaminius; viz., Neptune, Thetis, and her son Achilles; the Sea-nymphs, or Nereids, mounted upon dolphins, whales, and mighty sea-horses. . . .

Stevens wrote that "This observation, of course, is reminiscent of Browning's 'Neptune, though,/Taming a sea-horse.' But Scopas belongs to classical antiquity and can by no means be historically related to the events in question. I propose, however, that Browning was thoroughly familiar with these pages in the book for which he avows a fondness, and that the two incidents—one of the duke of Ferrara's skillful portrait painter,

the other of the skillful sculptor of marine-myth figures—being
placed in close proximity to one another [presumably, "close"
in both poem and palazzo], were subconsciously related in the
poet's mind, and that they provide the germ for the observations
with which Browning gets us into and then out of his famous
monologue. Frà Pandolf and Claus of Innsbruck have hitherto
been considered pure fictions; they are perhaps more accurately
seen as the imaginative germinations of historical seeds. The
degree of change that the stories undergo suggests that they
merely prompt the two pertinent allusions and then give way
to the vigorous imagination of the poet. It was perhaps this
freedom of imagination that enabled Browning to rearrange
these little fragments from Wanley into a new, dramatic whole
and hence to achieve the sort of independence from his sources
that was ultimately to give *The Ring and the Book* its unique
tension between history and the imagination." [243]

The Name "Pandolf"

The Italian name Pandolfo has been anglicized to "Pandolf," since to both men, the Duke and the emissary, who are Italian, there would of course be nothing 'foreign' or 'exotic' about the painter's name. This practice of Browning's, although occasionally annoying—especially when the reader confronts quite familiar names in slightly transposed forms—seems nonetheless reasonable enough. Such other instances that might be cited could include "St. Praxed" (Santa Prassede), "Leonard" (-o), "George" (Giorgio) Vasari, "John of Douay" (Giambologna, or Giovanni da Bologna, or Jean de Bologne; in *The Statue and the Bust*), "John of the Black Bands" (Giovanni delle Bande Nere), and so forth. However, in *Up in a Villa—Down in the City*, "Petrarca" appears as himself rather than in the usual English guise of 'Petrarch'; and *The Ring and the Book* preserves most of the Italian names—e.g., "San Giovanni," "Pietro," "Girolamo"—intact.

Perhaps it might be mentioned that 'Pandolfo,' by no means a common name in Renaissance Italy, has a number of interesting connections. First, Pandolfo Collenuccio of Pesaro was a humanist who, at the invitation of Ercole I (great-grandfather of Alfonso II) wrote a history of the kingdom of Naples.[244] Collenuccio was also sponsored by Eleanora d'Aragona, Ercole I's Duchess, in letters and dramatic productions.[245] Second, Gustave Gruyer cited one Pandolfo da Pesaro as a silversmith for Ludovico Sforza (il Moro, Duke of Milan, who married

Beatrice d'Este, sister of Alfonso I, who was the grandfather of Alfonso II): *"Plusieurs médailles d'argent avaient été offertes au duc par Monseigneur d'Adria et par Pandolfo da Pesaro."* [246]

Third, Friedland mentioned a Giovanni Antonio Pandolfi, who "in 1570, on the occasion of a festive reception given in Pesaro for the entry of Lucrezia d'Este (Alfonso's *sister*), . . . painted a large portrait of her for one of the triumphal arches. This, of course, was long after Lucrezia de' Medici's death." [247]

Fourth, the 1805 edition of Pilkington's *A Dictionary of Painters* mentioned only one Pandolfo.[248] This was Pandolfo Reschi (ca. 1643–1699), an imitator of Salvatore Rosa and Giacomo Borgognone notable for his battle scenes, architectural views and perspectives, and landscapes. The 1824 edition of Pilkington's *A General Dictionary of Painters* listed, in addition to Reschi,[249] Giangiacomo Pandolfi (fl. ca. 1640), an imitator of Federigo Zucchero who lived in Pesaro and painted mainly religious subjects; he might have been related to Lucrezia d'Este's celebrant Giovanni Antonio Pandolfi.[250] The 1770 edition of Pilkington's *The Gentleman's and Connoisseur's Dictionary of Painters* mentioned only "Pandolfo, or Reschi." [251] The name, then, could not be a more recondite one for an Italian artist.

The fifth item of peripheral note is that Pandolfo is the middle name of Sigismondo Malatesta (1417–1468), a strong Emilian *condottiere* whose rule extended to Ferrara. The Malatesta family in general seemed to favor the name.[252] Ancestors of Sigismondo Pandolfo Malatesta include Gianciotto Malatesta, who murdered his brother Paolo and his wife (and beloved of Paolo), Francesca da Rimini; and Parisina Malatesta, imprisoned in a dungeon and later executed by her husband Nicolò III (a Duke of Ferrara, and the father of Ercole I) together with his stepson and her lover, Ugo.[253] But one hesitates to make too firm a connection between these murders of erring wives by (jealous) husbands and the situation of Browning's Duke.

APPENDIX D

Notes

1. Howard, "The Dramatic Monologue: Its Origin and Development," p. 35.
2. Fuson, *Browning and His English Predecessors in the Dramatic Monolog*, p. 22; italics Fuson's.
3. Corson, "The Idea of Personality, as Embodied in Robert Browning's Poetry," p. 53.
4. Howard, *ibid.*, p. 86.
5. Honan, *Browning's Characters: A Study in Poetic Technique*, pp. 109–111.
6. Griffin and Minchin, *The Life of Robert Browning*, p. 133.
7. Fuson, *Browning and His English Predecessors in the Dramatic Monolog*, p. 9.
8. Alexander, *An Introduction to the Poetry of Robert Browning*, p. 9.
9. Palmer, "The Monologue of Browning," pp. 130–131.
10. Charlton, "Browning: The Making of the Dramatic Lyric," p. 349.
11. Blackburn, *Robert Browning: A Study of His Poetry*, p. 137. See also Watts and Watts, *A Dictionary of English Literature*, p. 353; Curry, *Browning and the Dramatic Monologue*; Langbaum, *The Poetry of Experience: The Dramatic Monologue in Modern Literary Tradition*, especially chapters I, II, and IV; Sessions, "The Dramatic Monologue," especially pp. 508–510; Anon., Review of the 1849 edition of Browning's *Poems*, pp. 211–213; and Baker, *Browning's Shorter Poems*, p. xiii.
12. Bryson, *Robert Browning*, p. 70.
13. Wenger, "The Masquerade in Browning's Dramatic Monologues," p. 227.
14. Wenger, *ibid.*, p. 235.
15. Wenger, *ibid.*, p. 238.
16. Wenger, *loc. cit.*
17. Wade, "My Last Duchess," in *Plays from Browning*, p. 43.

18. Wade, *loc. cit.*
19. Wade, *ibid.,* p. 41.
20. Wade, *ibid.,* pp. 46–47.
21. Wade, *ibid.,* pp. 50–51.
22. Anon., "The Poetry of Robert Browning," p. 438.
23. Jones, "Browning as a Dramatic Poet," p. 19.
24. Jones, *ibid.,* p. 16.
25. Jones, *ibid.,* p. 20.
26. Jones, *ibid.,* p. 15.
27. Jones, *ibid.,* p. 17.
28. Jones, *ibid.,* p. 23.
29. MacCallum, "The Dramatic Monologue in the Victorian Period," pp. 276–277.
30. Grant, "Browning's Art in Monologue," pp. 65–66. See also Gleason, *The Dramatic Art of Robert Browning,* pp. 64–84.
31. Fairchild, "Browning the Simple-Hearted Casuist," p. 225.
32. Wenger, "The Masquerade in Browning's Dramatic Monologues," p. 227.
33. Palmer, "The Monologue of Browning," pp. 140–141.
34. Palmer, *ibid.,* p. 133.
35. Langbaum, *The Poetry of Experience: The Dramatic Monologue in Modern Literary Tradition,* p. 85.
36. Langbaum, *ibid.,* p. 83.
37. Langbaum, *ibid.,* p. 86.
38. Cadbury, "Lyric and Anti-Lyric Forms: A Method for Judging Browning," p. 34.
39. Cadbury, *loc. cit.*
40. Routh, *Towards the Twentieth Century: Essays in the Spiritual History of the Nineteenth,* p. 102.
41. See, e.g., Griffin and Minchin, *The Life of Robert Browning,* pp. 94–103.
42. Griffin and Minchin, *ibid.,* p. 102.
43. Griffin and Minchin, *ibid.,* pp. 101–102.
44. See also Burton, "Renaissance Pictures in Robert Browning's Poetry," p. 70.
45. Latimer, "A Browning Monologue," p. 183.
46. Boulton, "Browning—A Potential Revolutionary," p. 175.
47. Friedland, "Ferrara and *My Last Duchess,*" p. 684.
48. Sharp, *Life of Robert Browning,* p. 129.
49. Curry, *Browning and the Dramatic Monologue,* p. 99.
50. Blackburn, *Robert Browning: A Study of His Poetry,* p. 173.

51. Symons, *An Introduction to the Study of Browning*, p. 60.

52. The name is used here only for body natural convenience, as "Lucrezia" will be.

53. See also Perrine, "Browning's Shrewd Duke," pp. 377–378.

54. Like most of the great Renaissance Italian families (the Medici, the Sforza, Gonzaga, della Rovere, Farnese, Gritti, Schiavone, Strozzi, and others), the Este of Ferrara were notable sponsors and patrons of many great artists—in painting and sculpture, Iacopo and Giovanni Bellini, Michelangelo, Mantegna, Tiziano, Rogier van der Weyden, Pisanello, Piero della Francesca, Benvenuto Cellini, Cosimo Tura, Raffaello, Dosso Dossi, Francia, Ercole Roberti, and Francesco del Cossa (whose titanic *Due Mesi di Schifanoia* murals remain in the Saletta dei Giochi, the Small Gameroom, in the Castello Schifanoia in Ferrara), among others; in music, Palestrina, Josquin des Prez, Adriano Willaert, and Johannes Ockeghem; in letters, Boiardo, Ariosto, Castiglione, and Tasso. (See Solerti, *Ferrara e la Corte Estense nella Seconda Metà del Secolo Decimosesto*, chapters I–II and VIII; Chiappini, *Gli Estensi* and *Eleanora d'Aragona, Prima Duchessa di Ferrara*; and Cittadella, *Il Castello di Ferrara*.) Of these masters, Alfonso II was the personal patron of Palestrina, Ockeghem, Tasso, Tiziano, and Giovanni Bellini. But Ercole I was possibly the most notable art patron of the family; he commissioned Mantegna to paint the celebrated *Madonna con Figlio e Cherubini* (now in the Brera in Milan) and Cosimo Tura to paint portraits of many members of his family. (See Chiappini, *Gli Estensi*, Chapter VII, and *Eleanora d'Aragona*, p. 45.)

55. Pipes, "The Portrait of 'My Last Duchess,'" pp. 384–385.

56. As has been noted, Browning had not been to Ferrara up to the time of the composition of the poem, but he had been in other northern Italian cities with huge palazzi, and he might in addition have seen illustrations of the interiors of yet other Renaissance homes of vast dimensions—e.g., those of Florence, Milan, and Rome.

57. Pipes, *ibid.*, p. 384.

58. Perrine, "Browning's Shrewd Duke," p. 340.

59. Beatty (*Browning's Verse Form: Its Organic Character*, p. 25) called attention to the alliterative linking, "which has a fusing effect on the whole line," of lines 2 and 3:

> Looking as if she were alive.
> I call,

to which might be added the first line as well:

> . . . painted on the wall,
> Looking. . . .

Beatty also noted the same effect in lines 18 and 19:

> . . . the faint
> Half-flush that dies along her throat.

60. Dowden, *Robert Browning*, p. 79.
61. Assad, "Browning's 'My Last Duchess,' " p. 119.
62. Millet, "Art and Reality in 'My Last Duchess,' " pp. 25–26.
63. See, for example, Crowell, *The Triple Soul: Browning's Theory of Knowledge*, p. 172; Rogers, *The Best of Browning*, p. 518; Pipes, "The Portrait of 'My Last Duchess,' " p. 384; Jerman, "Browning's Witless Duke," pp. 332–333 (cf. Perrine, "Browning's Shrewd Duke," p. 341), etc.
64. Our authority here is Professor Howard McP. Davis, of the Department of Art History, Columbia University, in conversation.
65. Crowell, *ibid.*, p. 172.
66. Zamwalt, "Christian Symbolism in 'My Last Duchess.' "
67. Kilburn, "Browning's *My Last Duchess.*"
68. Assad, "Browning's 'My Last Duchess,' " pp. 118–119.
69. Friedland, "Ferrara and *My Last Duchess*," p. 678.
70. Friedland, *ibid.*, p. 662.
71. Burrows, *Browning the Poet: An Introductory Study*, p. 116.
72. Burrows, *ibid.*, p. 117.
73. Alexander, *An Introduction to the Poetry of Robert Browning*, pp. 11–12.
74. See Brockington, "Robert Browning's Answers to Questions concerning Some of His Poems," p. 317.
75. Matthew Pilkington was an Eighteenth Century compiler of brief biographical and critical sketches of painters; his major compilations include the 1770 *The Gentleman's and Connoisseur's Dictionary of Painters*, the 1805 *A Dictionary of Painters*, and the 1824 *A General Dictionary of Painters* (see Appendices A, B, and C). Browning referred to these works—especially *A Dictionary of Painters*—constantly; and the Pilkington works became the source "from . . . which most of his early knowledge of the history of art was gained" and the "influence of [which] is plainly traceable in his work" (Griffin and Minchin, *The Life of Robert Browning*, p. 15).
76. Millet, "Art and Reality in 'My Last Duchess,' " p. 25.
77. See also Monteiro, "Browning's 'My Last Duchess,' " p. 235.

78. Mayne, *Browning's Heroines*, p. 171.

79. Mayne, *ibid.*, p. 173.

80. Mayne, *ibid.*, pp. 174–175; the suggestive and outraged ellipsis marks are Miss Mayne's. See also Davison, "Browning's Portraits of Women," pp. 352–353.

81. Chesterton, *Robert Browning*, pp. 83–85.

82. See also Whitman, "Robert Browning in His Relation to the Art of Painting."

83. Whitla, *The Central Truth: The Incarnation in Browning's Poetry*, p. 57.

84. Whitla, *loc. cit.*; cf. Howling, "Browning's Theory of the Purpose of Art," which is a more generalized study of art as revelation of "truth."

85. Dowden, *Robert Browning*, pp. 78–79.

86. Hofgrefe, *Browning and Italian Art and Artists*, p. 13; her italics.

87. Hofgrefe, *ibid.*, p. 42.

88. Hofgrefe, *ibid.*, p. 54; see also Harris, "Studies in Browning's Art Poems," p. 349.

89. Williams, *Robert Browning*, p. 94.

90. Buckley, *The Victorian Temper: A Study in Literary Culture*, p. 215.

91. Pipes, "The Portrait of 'My Last Duchess,' " p. 386.

92. Seaman, "Browning's Attitude towards Art and Nature," p. 109.

93. Langbaum, *The Poetry of Experience: The Dramatic Monologue in Modern Literary Tradition*, p. 83.

94. Stevens, "Aestheticism in Browning's Early Renaissance Monologues," p. 20.

95. Assad, "Browning's 'My Last Duchess,' " p. 121.

96. Assad, *ibid.*, p. 122.

97. Johnson, *The Alien Vision of Victorian Poetry*, p. 111.

98. Monteiro, "Browning's 'My Last Duchess,' " p. 236.

99. See also Kirk and McCutcheon, *An Introduction to the Study of Poetry*, p. 22.

100. One commentator saw the entire relationship between Duke and Duchess writ small in "that spot of joy." The phrase, he found, is ample Ducal disparagement of the lady, since it is "symbolic of a lack of taste, vanity, sensuous passion or of selfishness. . . . In the Duke's description of this example of the spot appearing ["Fràt Pandolf's" "courtesy"], he seems to think that the Duchess has poor taste, that she displays a lack of intelligence and that she is vain." (Cox, "The 'Spot of Joy' in 'My Last Duchess,' " p. 72.) But for any other besides the Duke, "The phrase 'spot of joy' is a figure which spreads a montage-like passing through the mind's eye of sensuous images, love

of life and humanity, intellectual awareness, artistic merit, lack of
taste, vanity, and possibly, selfishness." (Cox, *loc. cit.*)

101. Cf. *Hamlet* II.ii.585–586:

> What's Hecuba to him or he to Hecuba,
> That he should weep for her?

102. Assad, "Browning's 'My Last Duchess,' " p. 123; cf. Cox, *ibid.*, p. 73.
103. Boulton, "Browning—A Potential Revolutionary," p. 175.
104. Beatty, *Browning's Verse Form: Its Organic Character,* p. 24.
105. Perrine, "Browning's Shrewd Duke," p. 338.
106. Assad, "Browning's 'My Last Duchess,' " p. 126.
107. Assad, *ibid.*, p. 124.
108. Bates, *Browning Critiques,* pp. 83–84.
109. Chesterton, *Robert Browning,* p. 27.
110. Perrine, "Browning's Shrewd Duke," p. 340.
111. Brockington, *Browning and the Twentieth Century,* p. 122.
112. Rolfe, "Browning's Mastery of Rhyme," p. 167.
113. Phelps, *Robert Browning,* pp. 171–173.
114. Hatcher, *The Versification of Robert Browning,* p. 142.
115. Beatty, *Browning's Verse Form: Its Organic Character,* p. 22.
116. Beatty, *ibid.*, p. 24.
117. Smith, *Browning's Star-Imagery,* p. 140.
118. Burrow's, *Browning: An Introductory Essay,* p. 39.
119. Burrows, *Browning the Poet: An Introductory Study,* pp. 116–117.
120. Beatty, *Browning's Verse Form: Its Organic Character,* p. 25. See also
    Melchiori, *Browning's Poetry of Reticence,* p. 8; and Blackburn,
    Robert Browning: A Study of His Poetry, p. 43.
121. The caesurae here, and throughout the poem, "give an arrested move-
    ment and broken flow expressive of the cruel tragedy which crushed
    that joyous life." (Beatty, *ibid.*, p. 24.)
122. Burrows, *Browning the Poet: An Introductory Study,* p. 118.
123. Burrows, *loc. cit.*
124. See *Hamlet* I.iii.16–24:

> But you must fear
> His greatness weighed, his will is not his own,
> For he himself is subject to his birth.
> He may not, as unvalued persons do,
> Carve for himself, for on his choice depends
> The safety and health of this whole state,

And therefore must his choice be circumscribed
Unto the voice and yielding of that body
Whereof he is the head.

125. Russell, *One Word More on Browning*, p. 24.
126. DeVane, *A Browning Handbook*, p. 109.
127. DeVane, *loc. cit.*
128. Corson, *An Introduction to the Study of Robert Browning's Poetry*, pp. 87–88; cf. the outraged and anonymous critic of *Poet Lore*, I, 11, p. 569.
129. Friedland, "Ferrara and *My Last Duchess*," pp. 676–677.
130. Friedland, *ibid.*, p. 676n.
131. See, e.g., Langbaum, *The Poetry of Experience: The Dramatic Monologue in Modern Literary Tradition*, p. 82; Russell, *One Word More on Browning*, p. 24; Kirk and McCutcheon, *An Introduction to the Study of Poetry*, pp. 20–21; Porter and Clarke, eds., *The Complete Works of Robert Browning*, Vol. IV, p. 384; "E. J. H.," "Browning's Poems"; and Rogers, *The Best of Browning*, pp. 518–519.
132. Brooks, Purser, and Warren, *An Approach to Literature*, p. 295.
133. Curry, *Browning and the Dramatic Monologue*, p. 99.
134. Burrows, *Browning: An Introductory Essay*, p. 40.
135. Alexander, *An Introduction to the Poetry of Robert Browning*, pp. 10–11.
136. Fleissner, "Browning's Last Lost Duchess: A Purview," p. 218.
137. Fleissner, *ibid.*, p. 217.
138. Fleissner, *ibid.*, pp. 217–218.
139. Fleissner, *ibid.*, pp. 218–219.
140. Stevenson, " 'My Last Duchess' and *Parisinia*," p. 490.
141. Blackburn, *Robert Browning: A Study of His Poetry*, p. 61.
142. Howard, "The Dramatic Monologue: Its Origin and Development," p. 70.
143. See Nathanson, "Browning's *My Last Duchess*."
144. Assad, "Browning's 'My Last Duchess,' " p. 127; cf. Alexander, *An Introduction to the Study of Robert Browning*, p. 14.
145. Burrows, *Browning the Poet: An Introductory Study*, p. 115.
146. Brooks, Purser, and Warren, *An Approach to Literature*, p. 295.
147. Brooks, Purser, and Warren, *loc. cit.*
148. Langbaum, *The Poetry of Experience: The Dramatic Monologue in Modern Literary Tradition*, p. 82.
149. Perrine, "Browning's Shrewd Duke," p. 339.
150. Monteiro, "Browning's 'My Last Duchess,' " p. 235.

151. Perrine, *ibid.*, pp. 338–340.

152. Burrows, *Browning the Poet: An Introductory Study*, p. 120.

153. Corson believed the piece a much larger one than could be accommodated in a wall niche; hence, he found that these lines indicate "that on the stairway is a window which affords an outlook into the courtyard. . . ." (*An Introduction to Robert Browning's Poetry*, p. 90; see also Alexander, *An Introduction to the Poetry of Robert Browning*, p. 14.) The view taken here is that the piece was small, not more than two feet high, and more probably eighteen inches, such as are the bronzes of the Pollaiuoli, Giambologna, Pietro Tacca, Il Riccio, Sansovino, Baccio Bandinelli, Francesco da Sant'Agato, and Severo da Ravenna (see Appendix B).

154. Orr, *A Handbook to the Works of Robert Browning*, p. 251.

155. Monteiro, "Browning's 'My Last Duchess,' " pp. 235, 237.

156. The issue of the painter's primacy over the subject, or even his being of equal worth to that subject, seems somewhat out of Renaissance (even late Renaissance, *cinquecento*) context here, in those times the executioner of a painting or sculpture, including portraits and other likenesses, generally being considered quite a lesser matter than its subject. Those "youths" and "ladies" and "old men," the *ignote* and *ignoti,* had names and usually some current local celebrity. Now—and in Browning's time a century ago—the artist's identity is primary and the subject's name often forgotten or of concern only to the antiquarian; subsequent to the Renaissance, a work became less a double portrait of Jean de Dinteville and Georges de Selve (by Hans Holbein the Younger, court painter to Henry VIII) and more a Holbein (*The Ambassadors*) (see Appendix A).

157. Berdoe, *The Browning Cyclopaedia*, p. 282.

158. Friedland, "Ferrara and *My Last Duchess*," p. 682n.

159. Graves, *The Greek Myths,* Vol. One, p. 59.

160. Rose, *A Handbook of Greek Mythology*, p. 65.

161. Graves, *loc. cit.*

162. Rose, *ibid.,* p. 63.

163. Monteiro, "Browning's 'My Last Duchess,' " p. 236.

164. Spindler, *Robert Browning und Die Antike,* Vol. II, p. 130; the writer's translation.

165. Friedland, "Ferrara and *My Last Duchess*," p. 682.

166. See also Blackburn, *Robert Browning: A Study of His Poetry,* p. 174.

167. See also Nitchie, "Browning's 'Duchess.' "

168. McCormick, *As a Flame Springs*, pp. 219–220.

169. Cohen, *Robert Browning*, p. 30.

170. Sim, *Robert Browning: The Poet and the Man, 1833–1846*, p. 152.
171. Corson, *An Introduction to the Study of Robert Browning's Poetry*, pp. 86–90.
172. Herford, *Robert Browning*, pp. 66, 70.
173. Stedman, *Victorian Poets*, p. 321.
174. Skemp, *Robert Browning*, p. 59.
175. Kirk and McCutcheon, *An Introduction to the Study of Poetry*, p. 21.
176. Powell, *The Confessions of a Browning Lover*, p. 39.
177. Pridham, "Browning's Heroines," p. 62.
178. Berdoe, *The Browning Cyclopaedia*, p. 281.
179. Nathanson, "Browning's *My Last Duchess*."
180. Stevenson, " 'My Last Duchess' and *Parisina*," p. 492.
181. Blackburn, *Robert Browning: A Study of His Poetry*, p. 60.
182. Burrows, *Browning the Poet: An Introductory Study*, p. 119.
183. Gransden, "The Uses of Personae," p. 61.
184. Zamwalt, "Christian Symbolism in 'My Last Duchess.' "
185. Curry, *Browning and the Dramatic Monologue*, p. 98.
186. Burrows, *Browning the Poet: An Introductory Study*, pp. 118–119.
187. Phelps, *Robert Browning*, pp. 173–175.
188. Burrows, *ibid.*, p. 119.
189. Phelps, *ibid.*, pp. 173–174.
190. Brockington, *Browning and the Twentieth Century*, p. 122.
191. *Dramatic Lyrics* (1842) was the third part of *Bells and Pomegranates*. In these *Dramatic Lyrics* the poem now called *My Last Duchess* was printed with *Count Gismond* under the mutual heading *Italy and France*, the former poem being designated "I. Italy" and the latter "II. France." In the 1863 and 1868 *Poetical Works* the poem was given the title by which we now know it; in the former year *My Last Duchess* appeared with *The Romances*, in the latter year with *Dramatic Romances*. "Ferrara" was appended beneath the title in 1863 to designate the location of the action (and the identity of the speaker as well), as "Aix in Provence" was added to *Count Gismond*.

See also DeVane, *A Browning Handbook*, pp. 102, 103, and 107.
192. See Burton, "Renaissance Pictures in Robert Browning's Poetry."
193. Brooke, *The Poetry of Robert Browning*, p. 317.
194. Duffin, *Amphibian: A Reconsideration of Browning*, p. 176.
195. Duffin, *ibid.*, p. 177.
196. An isolated exception is Melchiori; see her *Browning's Poetry of Reticence*, p. 22n. Rea's article is entitled "My Last Duchess."
197. See Károly, *A Guide to the Paintings of Florence*, p. 108.
198. Friedland, "Ferrara and *My Last Duchess*," p. 670.

199. Friedland, *ibid.*, p. 673; cf. Clarke, *Browning's Italy: A Study of Italian Life and Art in Browning*, pp. 287–288.

200. Friedland, *loc. cit.*

201. Friedland, *loc. cit.*

202. Friedland, *ibid.*, p. 683.

203. Friedland, *ibid.*, p. 677.

204. Stevens, " 'My Last Duchess': A Possible Source," p. 25.

205. Stevens, *loc. cit.*

206. Stevens, *loc. cit.*

207. Stevens, *loc. cit.*

208. Stevens, *loc. cit.*

209. Stevens, *ibid.*, pp. 25–26.

210. Stevens, *ibid.*, p. 26.

211. Stevens, *loc. cit.*

212. Stevens, *ibid.*, p. 25.

213. See also Griffin and Minchin, *The Life of Robert Browning*, pp. 20–25; and Cook, *A Guide-Book to the Poetic and Dramatic Works of Robert Browning*, pp. 243 and 291.

214. Friedland, "Ferrara and *My Last Duchess*," p. 679.

215. See Muratori, *Annali d 'Italia*, Vol. IX, pp. 684 and 685; Muratori, *Delle Antichità Estensi ed Italiane*, Vol. I, Genealogical Table II; and Chiappini, *Gli Estensi*, pp. 15–20 and Genealogical Table II.

216. Muratori, *Annali d'Italia*, Vol. VII, p. 338; the writer's translation. That "elsewhere" is the *Antiquitates Italicae Medii Aevi*, Dissertation LXXX, pp. 469–471.

217. Muratori, *Delle Antichità Estensi ed Italiane*, Vol. I, Genealogical Table I; and Chiappini, *Gli Estensi*, Genealogical Table II.

218. Pieraccini, *La Stirpe de' Medici di Cafaggiolo*, Vol. II, p. 96; the writer's translation. See also Solerti, *Ferrara e la Corte Estense nella Seconda Metà del Secolo Decimosesto*, p. xxvii.

219. Chiappini, *Gli Estensi*, pp. 284–285; the writer's translation.

220. See Chiappini, *ibid.*, pp. 285, 286, 287, 296, 297, 299, 306, 310, and 311; Solerti, *ibid.*, pp. xxvii and xxxiii; Noyes, *The Story of Ferrara*, p. 244; Muratori, *Annali d'Italia*, Vol. XV, pp. 138–140; and Muratori, *Delle Antichità Estensi ed Italiane*, Vol. II, pp. 268ff.

221. See Chiappini, *ibid.*, Genealogical Table XIV.

222. Pieraccini, *La Stirpe de' Medici di Cafaggiolo*, pp. 93–94.

223. See Chiappini, *ibid.*, pp. 290ff; Solerti, *loc. cit.*; and Sardi, *Libro delle Historie Ferraresi*, Part II, Book II, pp. 88–102. Alfonso died on 27 October 1597, not 1598 as Friedland reported ("Ferrara and *My Last Duchess*," p. 683).

224. Anon., "Unique Poems." For more on this item, see Greer, *Browning and America*, pp. 30 and 224–225.

225. Friedland, *ibid.*, pp. 667–678. See also Gruyer, *L'Art Ferrarais a l'Epoque des Princes d'Este*, Vol. I, pp. 339 and 409, and Vol. II, p. 391; and Williamson, ed., *Bryan's Dictionary of Painters*, Vol. II, pp. 140–141.

226. Friedland, *ibid.*, p. 678.

227. Solerti, *Ferrara e la Corte Estense nella Seconda Metà del Secolo Decimosesto*, p. ix, n.1. See also Sardi, *Libro delle Historie Ferraresi*, which contains reproductions of what might have been some of the Faccini portraits in the mid-Seventeenth Century, when they were already in poor condition.

228. Pilkington, *The Gentleman's and Connoisseur's Dictionary of Painters*, pp. 205–206; *A Dictionary of Painters*, p. 182; and *A General Dictionary of Painters*, Vol. I, pp. 307–308.

229. See Bazzi, *The Artist's Methods and Materials*, pp. 181–182.

230. See Bellei, *Sposizione delle Pitture in Muro*.

231. McComb, *Agnolo Bronzino: His Life and Works*, p. 94. See also Schulze, *Die Werke Angelo Bronzinos*, p. xii; and Pieraccini, *La Stirpe de' Medici di Cafaggiolo*, Vol. II, p. 90, Plate LXVI.

232. Smyth, *Bronzino Studies*, pp. 135ff.

233. See Chiappini, *Gli Estensi*, opposite p. 288.

234. See Frizzi, *Album Estense*, opposite p. 146.

235. See Gibbons, *Dosso and Battista Dossi, Court Painters at Ferrara*, p. 249 and Figure 192; and Mezzetti, *Il Dosso e Battista Ferrarese*, p. 94.

236. See Cittadella, *Documenti ed Illustrazione risguardanti la Storia Artistica Ferrarese*, p. 161.

237. See Armand, *Les Médailleurs Italiens*, Vol. I, pp. 193, 195, 212, and 260; Vol. II, pp. 193, 194, 195, and 296; and Vol. III, pp. 84 and 245. See also Hill, *Renaissance Medals from the Samuel H. Kress Collection at the National Gallery of Art*, pp. 61 and 63; and Fabriczy, *Italian Medals*, p. 149 and Plate XXXI, No. 2.

238. See Anon., *Paintings and Sculpture from the Widener Collection*, p. 144.

239. See Pope-Hennessy and Radcliffe, *The Frick Collection: An Illustrated Catalogue*, Vol. III: *Sculpture*, pp. 126–135; and Perkins, *Historical Handbook of Italian Sculpture*, pp. 365–366.

240. See Anon., *Italian Bronze Statuettes*, Item 147, Plate xxv; and Cessi, *Alessandro Vittoria, Bronzista*, pp. 41, 42, 44, and 73–77, and Plates 5, 6, 7, and 8.

241. See Medri, *I Bronzi Artistici del Civico Museo Schifanoia: Catologo,* p. 19; and Hermann, "Pier Jacopo Alari-Bonacolsi gennant Antico," p. 216.

242. Friedland, "Ferrara and *My Last Duchess,*" pp. 682–683.

243. Stevens, " 'My Last Duchess': A Possible Source," p. 26.

244. See Chiappini, *Eleanora d'Aragona, Prima Duchessa di Ferrara,* p. 45.

245. See Gruyer, *L'Art Ferrarais a l'Epoque des Princes d'Este,* Vol. I, pp. 75 and 110; and Vol. II, p. 530.

246. Gruyer, *ibid.,* Vol. I, p. 89n.

247. Friedland, "Ferrara and *My Last Duchess,*" p. 678n.

248. Pilkington, *A Dictionary of Painters,* p. 437.

249. Pilkington, *A General Dictionary of Painters,* Vol. II, p. 232.

250. Pilkington, *ibid.,* Vol. II, p. 128.

251. Pilkington, *The Gentleman's and Connoisseur's Dictionary of Painters,* p. 443.

252. See Zama, *I Malatesta,* pp. 211ff; and Hutton, *Sigismondo Pandolfo Malatesta.*

253. See Stevenson's brief comparison of certain incidents in Byron's *Parisina* and Browning's *My Last Duchess.*

References Cited

Alexander, William John. *An Introduction to the Poetry of Robert Browning*. Boston, 1889.

Anon. *Italian Bronze Statuettes: An Exhibition Organised by the Arts Council of Great Britain with the Italian Ministry of Education and the Rijksmuseum, Amsterdam. Victoria and Albert Museum, London, 27 July–1 October, 1961*. London, 1961.

Anon. *Paintings and Sculpture from the Widener Collection*. Washington, 1959.

Anon. "Unique Poems," *The Literary World*, No. 136 (Sept. 8, 1849).

Anon. Review of 1849 edition of Browning's *Poems, Eclectic Review*, Series 4, Vol. 26, Article VII (August 1849), 203–214.

Anon. (no title) *Poet Lore*, Vol. I, No. 11 (1889), 569.

Anon. (E. P. Hood?) "The Poetry of Robert Browning," *The Eclectic Review*, New Series, Vol. IV (May 1863), 436–454.

Armand, Alfred. *Les Médailleurs Italiens*. Paris, 1883, and Bologna, 1968.

Assad, Thomas J. "Browning's 'My Last Duchess,'" *Tulane Studies in English*, Vol. X (1960), 117–128.

Baker, Franklin T., ed. *Browning's Shorter Poems*. New York, 1899.

Bates, Margaret H. *Browning Critiques*. Chicago, 1921

Bazzi, Maria. *The Artist's Methods and Materials*. (trans. by Francesca Priuli) London, 1960.

Beatty, Arthur. *Browning's Verse Form: Its Organic Character*. Unpublished Columbia University dissertation, 1897.

Bellei, Domenico. *Sposizione delle Pitture in Muro del Ducale Palazzo nella Nobil Terra di Sassuolo Grandiosa Villeggiature de' Serenissimi Principi Estensi*. Modena, 1784.

Berdoe, Edward. *The Browning Cyclopaedia*. London, 1892.

Blackburn, Thomas. *Robert Browning: A Study of His Poetry*. London, 1967.

Boulton, J. A. "Browning—A Potential Revolutionary," *Essays in Criticism*, Vol. III, 1953, 165–176.

Brockington, A. Allen. *Browning and the Twentieth Century*. New York, 1963 (first published 1932).

———. "Robert Browning's Answers to Questions concerning Some of His Poems," *The Cornhill Magazine*, New Series XXXVI (March 1914), 316–319.

Brooke, Stopford A. *The Poetry of Robert Browning*. New York, 1902.

Brooks, Cleanth, John Thibaut Purser, and Robert Penn Warren, eds. *An Approach to Literature*. New York, 1964 (fourth edition).

Bryson, John. *Robert Browning*. London, 1959.

Buckley, Jerome Hamilton. *The Victorian Temper: A Study in Literary Culture*. New York, 1964 (first published 1951).

Burrows, Leonard. *Browning: An Introductory Essay*. Perth, Australia, 1952.

————. *Browning the Poet: An Introductory Study*. Nedlands, Australia, 1969.

Burton, Richard. "Renaissance Pictures in Robert Browning's Poetry," *Poet Lore*, Vol. X, No. 1 (1898), 66–76.

Cadbury, William. "Lyric and Anti-Lyric Forms: A Method for Judging Browning," in Clarence Tracy, ed. *Browning's Mind and Art*, Edinburgh and London, 1968. 32–50.

Cessi, Francesco. *Alessandro Vittoria, Bronzista*. Trento, 1960.

Charlton, H. B. "Browning: The Making of the Dramatic Lyric," *Bulletin of the John Rylands Library*, XXXV (1953), 349–384.

Chesterton, Gilbert Keith. *Robert Browning*. New York, 1912 (ninth edition).

Chiappini, Luciano. *Eleanora d'Aragona, Prima Duchessa di Ferrara*. Ferrara, 1956.

————. *Gli Estensi*. Milano, 1967.

Cittadella, Luigi Napoleone. *Il Castello di Ferrara*. Ferrara, 1875.

————. *Documenti ed Illustrazione risguardanti la Storia Artistica Ferrarese*. Ferrara, 1868.

Clarke, Helen Archibald. *Browning's Italy: A Study of Italian Life and Art in Browning*. New York, 1907.

Cohen, J. M. *Robert Browning*. London, 1952.

Cook, George Willis. *A Guide-Book to the Poetic and Dramatic Works of Robert Browning*. Boston, 1891.

Corson, Hiram. *An Introduction to the Study of Robert Browning's Poetry*. Boston, 1889.

————. "The Idea of Personality, as Embodied in Robert Browning's Poetry," in Edward Berdoe, ed. *Browning Studies: Being Selected Papers by Members of the Browning Society*. London, 1895. 47–75.

Cox, Ollie. "The 'Spot of Joy' in 'My Last Duchess,' " *College Language Association Journal*, Vol. 12 (1968), 70–76.

Crowell, Norton B. *The Triple Soul: Browning's Theory of Knowledge*. Albuquerque, New Mexico, 1963.

Curry, S. S. *Browning and the Dramatic Monologue*. New York, 1965 (first published 1908).

Davison, W. T. "Browning's Portraits of Women," *The Living Age*, Seventh Series, Vol. LXIII (May 9, 1914), 352–356.

DeVane, William Clyde. *A Browning Handbook*. New York, 1955 (second edition).

Dowden, Edward. *Robert Browning*. London, 1904 (second edition).

Duffin, Henry Charles. *Amphibian: A Reconsideration of Browning*. London, 1956.

Fabriczy, Cornelius von. *Italian Medals*. London, 1904.

Fairchild, Hoxie N. "Browning the Simple-Hearted Casuist," in Boyd Litzinger and K. L. Knickerbocker, eds. *The Browning Critics*. Lexington, Kentucky, 1967. 218–228. (Reprinted from *The University of Toronto Quarterly*, XLVIII [April 1949] 234–240.)

Fleissner, R. F. "Browning's Last Lost Duchess: A Purview," *Victorian Poetry*, Vol. V, No. 3 (Autumn 1967), 217–219.

Friedland, Louis S. "Ferrara and *My Last Duchess*," *Studies in Philology*, Vol. 33 (1936), 656–684.

Frizzi, Antonio. *Album Estense*. Ferrara, 1850.

Fuson, Benjamin Willis. *Browning and His English Predecessors in the Dramatic Monolog*. *State University of Iowa Humanistic Studies*, Vol. VIII (1948).

Gibbons, Felton. *Dosso and Battista Dossi: Court Painters at Ferrara*. Princeton, 1968.

Gleason, Katherine Florence. *The Dramatic Art of Robert Browning*. Boston, 1927.

Gransden, K. W. "The Uses of Personae," in Clarence Tracy, ed. *Browning's Mind and Art*. Edinburgh and London, 1968. 51–74.

Grant, Percy Stickney. "Browning's Art in Monologue," in *The Boston Browning Society Papers*. New York, 1897. 35–66.

Graves, Robert. *The Greek Myths*. Baltimore, 1961 (fourth edition).

Greer, Louise. *Browning and America*. Chapel Hill, North Carolina, 1952.

Griffin, W. Hall, and Harry Christopher Minchin. *The Life of Robert Browning*. New York, 1910.

Gruyer, Gustave. *L'Art Ferrarais a l'Epoque des Princes D'Este*. Paris, 1897.

"E. J. H." "Browning's Poems," *St. Paul's Magazine*, Vol. VII (October 1870–March 1871), 264.

Harris, Roy. "Studies in Browning's Art Poems," *McMaster University Monthly*, Vol. XXVII (May 1918), 349–358.

Hatcher, Harlan Henthorne. *The Versification of Robert Browning.* Columbus, Ohio, 1928.

Herford, Charles H. *Robert Browning.* New York, 1905.

Hermann, H. J. "Pier Jacopo Alari-Bonacolsi gennant Antico," *Jahrbuch der Kunsthistorisches Sammlungen in Wien,* Vol. XXVIII, No. 5 (1910).

Hill, G. F. *Renaissance Medals from the Samuel H. Kress Collection at the National Gallery of Art, Washington.* London, 1967.

Hofgrefe, Pearl. *Browning and Italian Art and Artists. Bulletin of the University of Kansas, Humanistic Studies,* Vol. I, No. 3 (1914).

Honan, Park. *Browning's Characters: A Study of Poetic Technique.* New Haven, 1962.

Howard, Claud. "The Dramatic Monologue: Its Origin and Development," *Studies in Philology,* Vol. IV (1910), 31–88.

Howling, Robert Tunis. "Browning's Theory of the Purpose of Art," *Susquehanna University Studies,* Vol. IV, No. 3 (Bulletin No. 2, Series XLVIII, April–June, 1951), 215–228.

Hutton, Edward. *Sigismondo Pandolfo Malatesta, Lord of Rimini.* London and New York, 1906.

Jerman, B. R. "Browning's Witless Duke," in Boyd Litzinger and K. L. Knickerbocker, eds. *The Browning Critics.* Lexington, Kentucky, 1967, 328–335. (Reprinted from *PMLA,* LXXII [June 1957] 488–493.)

Johnson, Edward D. H. *The Alien Vision of Victorian Poetry.* Princeton, 1952.

Jones, Henry. "Browning as a Dramatic Poet," *Poet Lore,* Vol. VI, No. 1 (1894), 13–28.

Károly, Karl. *A Guide to the Paintings of Florence.* London, 1893.

Kilburn, Patrick E. "Browning's *My Last Duchess,*" *The Explicator,* Vol. XIX, No. 5, Item 31 (February, 1961).

Kirk, Richard Ray, and Roger Philip McCutcheon. *An Introduction to the Study of Poetry.* New York, 1934.

Langbaum, Robert. *The Poetry of Experience: The Dramatic Monologue in Modern Literary Tradition.* New York, 1957.

Latimer, George Dimmick. "A Browning Monologue," in *The Boston Browning Society Papers.* New York, 1897, 164–172.

MacCallum, M. W. "The Dramatic Monologue in the Victorian Period," *Proceedings of the British Academy* (1924–1925), 265–282.

Mayne, Ethel. *Browning's Heroines.* London, 1913.

McComb, Arthur. *Agnolo Bronzino: His Life and Works.* Cambridge, Mass., 1928.

McCormick, James Patton. *As a Flame Springs.* New York, 1940.

Medri, Gualtiero. *I Bronzi Artistichi del Civico Museo Schifanoia: Catologo.* Ferrara, 1933.

Melchiori, Barbara. *Browning's Poetry of Reticence.* Edinburgh and London, 1968.

Mezzetti, Amalia. *Il Dosso e Battista Ferrarese.* Milano, 1965.

Millet, Stanton. "Art and Reality in 'My Last Duchess,' " *Victorian Newsletter,* No. 17 (1960), 25–27.

Monteiro, George. "Browning's 'My Last Duchess,' " *Victorian Poetry,* Vol. I, No. 3 (August 1963), 234–237.

Muratori, Lodovico Antonio. *Annali d' Italia.* Milano, 1819–1821.

———. *Antiquitates Italicae Medii Aevi,* Vol. XIV of *Opera Omnia.* Arezzo, 1778.

———. *Delle Antichità Estensi ed Italiane.* Modena, 1717 (Vol. I) and 1740 (Vol. II).

Nathanson, Leonard. "Browning's *My Last Duchess,*" *The Explicator,* Vol. XIX, No. 9, Item 68 (June 1961).

Nitchie, Elizabeth. "Browning's 'Duchess,' " *Essays in Criticism,* Vol. III (1953), 475–476.

Noyes, Ella. *The Story of Ferrara.* London, 1904.

Orr, Mrs. Sutherland. *A Handbook to the Works of Robert Browning.* London, 1896 (seventh edition).

Palmer, George Herbert. "The Monologue of Browning," *Harvard Theological Review,* Vol. XI, No. 2 (April 1918), 121–144.

Perkins, Charles. *Historical Handbook of Italian Sculpture.* New York, 1883.

Perrine, Laurence. "Browning's Shrewd Duke," in Boyd Litzinger and K. L. Knickerbocker, eds. *The Browning Critics,* Lexington, Kentucky, 1967, 336–342. (Reprinted from *PMLA,* LXXIV [March 1959], 157–159.)

Phelps, William Lyon. *Robert Browning.* New York, 1968 (reprinted from 1932 edition; first published 1915).

Pieraccini, Gaetano. *La Stirpe de' Medici di Cafaggiolo.* Firenze, 1924–1925.

Pilkington, Matthew. *A Dictionary of Painters.* London, 1805.

———. *A General Dictionary of Painters.* London, 1824.

———. *The Gentleman's and Connoisseur's Dictionary of Painters.* London, 1770.

Pipes, B. N., Jr. "The Portrait of 'My Last Duchess,' " *Victorian Studies,* Vol. III, No. 4 (June 1960), 381–386.

Pope-Hennessy, John, and Anthony F. Radcliffe. *The Frick Collection: An Illustrated Catalogue.* New York, 1970.

Porter, Charlotte, and Helen Archibald Clarke, eds. *The Complete Works of Robert Browning*. New York, 1899.

Powell, John Walker. *The Confessions of a Browning Lover*. New York, 1918.

Pridham, M. R. "Browning's Heroines," in Alex Hill, ed. *Notes to the Pocket Volume of Selections from the Poems of Robert Browning*. London, 1913, 59–65.

Rea, John D. "My Last Duchess," *Studies in Philology*, Vol. 29 (1932), 120–122.

Rogers, William Hudson. *The Best of Browning*. New York, 1942.

Rolfe, William J. "Browning's Mastery of Rhyme," in *The Boston Browning Society Papers*. New York, 1897, 164–172.

Rose, H. J. *A Handbook of Greek Mythology*. New York, 1959.

Routh, H. V. *Towards the Twentieth Century: Essays in the Spiritual History of the Nineteenth*. New York, 1937.

Russell, Frances T. *One Word More on Browning*. Stanford, 1927.

Sardi, Gasparo. *Libro delle Historie Ferraresi*. Ferrara, 1646.

Seaman, Owen. "Browning's Attitude Towards Art and Nature," in Alex Hill, ed. *Notes to the Pocket Volume of Selections from the Poems of Robert Browning*. London, 1913, 107–114.

Schulze, Hanns. *Die Werke Angelo Bronzinos*. Strassburg, 1911.

Sessions, Ina Beth. "The Dramatic Monologue," *PMLA*, Vol. LXII, No. 2 (June 1947), 503–516.

Sharp, William. *Life of Robert Browning*. London, 1897.

Sim, Frances M. *Robert Browning: The Poet and the Man, 1833–1846*. New York, 1923.

Skemp, A. R. *Robert Browning*. London, 1916.

Smith, C. Willard. *Browning's Star-Imagery*. New York, 1965 (first published 1941).

Smyth, Craig Hugh. *Bronzino Studies*. Unpublished Princeton University dissertation, 1955.

Solerti, Angelo. *Ferrara e la Corte Estense nella Seconda Metà del Secolo Decimosesto*. Ferrara, 1899.

Spindler, Robert. *Robert Browning und Die Antike*, Vol. II. Leipzig, 1930.

Stedman, Edmund Clarence. *Victorian Poets*. Boston and New York, 1892 (twenty-first edition).

Stevens, L. Robert. "Aestheticism in Browning's Early Renaissance Monologues," *Victorian Poetry*, Vol. III, No. 1 (Winter 1965), 19–24.

———. " 'My Last Duchess': A Possible Source," *The Victorian Newsletter*, No. 28 (Fall 1965), 25–26.

Stevenson, Lionel. "'My Last Duchess' and *Parisina*," *Modern Language Notes*, Vol. LXXIV, No. 6 (June 1959), 489–492.

Symons, Arthur. *An Introduction to the Study of Browning*. London, 1906.

Wade, Leila A. *Plays from Browning*. Boston, 1923.

Watts, Homer A., and William W. Watts. *A Dictionary of English Literature*. New York, 1945.

Wenger, C. N. "The Masquerade in Browning's Dramatic Monologues," *College English*, Vol. III, No. 3 (1941), 225–239.

Whitla, William. *The Central Truth: The Incarnation in Browning's Poetry*. Toronto, 1963.

Whitman, Sarah W. "Robert Browning in His Relation to the Art of Painting," in *Papers of the Boston Browning Society*. Boston, 1889, 3–13.

Williams, Ioan M. *Robert Browning*. London, 1967.

Williamson, George C., ed. *Bryan's Dictionary of Painters*. London, 1930.

Zama, Piero. *I Malatesta*. Faenza, 1965.

Zamwalt, Eugene E. "Christian Symbolism in 'My Last Duchess,'" *Notes and Queries*, New Series Vol. 5, No. 10 (October 1958) (Vol. CCIII of Continuing Series), 446.